THE
FINANCIAL
VERSE

A COMMON SENSE APPROACH FOR YOUR MONEY

HARRY N. STOUT

Vertel Publishing

The FinancialVerse
Copyright © 2019 by Harry N. Stout

First Edition

Printed in the United States

ISBN-13: 978-1-64112-018-0
ISBN-10: 1-64112-018-5

TABLE OF CONTENTS

PLEASE READ BEFORE YOU PROCEED

The FinancialVerse has been written to present financial concepts, tax, and basic financial information and ideas in a condensed, simple-to-understand manner. This was done to educate the reader and allow the reader to obtain a general understanding of the key financial challenges and decisions they will face in their life's journey.

The FinancialVerse, its author, or affiliated companies have not received any sponsorship or compensation from any of the organizations referenced in this book.

References to specific tax regulations, dollar limits, or regulatory restrictions were current as of the time of publication. As is the case in our fast-moving world, things change. The reader should make sure they have the most current information before they choose to take action on a particular idea presented in this book.

Before making any major financial decision or taking related financial actions, it is suggested that the reader consult a qualified financial professional who has been licensed to provide this information, needed service, or sell the requested financial products.

This informational publication is designed to provide general information on the subjects covered. Pursuant to Internal Revenue Circular 230, it is not, however, intended to provide specific legal or tax advice and cannot be used to avoid tax penalties or to promote, market, or recommend any tax plan or arrangement. Please note that *The FinancialVerse*, its affiliated companies, and their representatives and employees do not give legal or tax advice. As written in this book, the reader is encouraged to consult a tax adviser or attorney on these matters.

Thank you for purchasing *The FinancialVerse* and investing in your financial literacy.

FOREWORD

The financial universe—or the FinancialVerse, as I call it—is made up of the knowledge, decisions, resources, risks, and tools an individual encounters in their life's financial journey. I believe most people, regardless of background and level of education, do not fundamentally understand the financial universe such that they can successfully navigate the key financial decisions and risks they will face in life. Being armed with at least a basic knowledge of what they will encounter and how to go about making informed decisions will enable the traveler to reach a level of success well beyond what they thought possible. This book presents that knowledge and a framework to help the reader understand what a financial life looks like.

Given our rapidly changing world, the revolution impacting work, lengthening life spans, and today's major economic trends, navigating the FinancialVerse is more difficult than ever before. To be successful in whatever stage of the financial life you find yourself, you must have an understanding of what you are looking to achieve. As Stephen Covey states in his book *The 7 Habits of Highly Effective People*, you must begin with the end in mind. It is never too late to get started on improving your knowledge of and relationship with money. You can improve your journey and make it more successful with that success defined by you.

THE VALUE OF THIS BOOK

Do you understand how money works? Have you achieved financial security for yourself and your family? Have you reached a point where you pay bills without thinking of whether you have enough in your bank account to cover the ATM withdrawal, check, or electronic payment? Do you have an up-to-date personal cash budget? Do you have the requisite insurance coverage in place to protect your family and property? Are financial issues *not* a daily part of your family discussions? Do you have enough savings to live the life you want in your older age? Do you have someone you can talk to about your money concerns? If the answer to most of these questions is no, you are failing in what I call the FinancialVerse—just like the majority of Americans.

It's time to become better aware of where you are in your life's financial journey and where you are headed. You should not fear this journey. It's all about common sense. You can make it work, but you must have a basic understanding and awareness of where you are and where you are headed.

I am here to help you by providing thoughts and ideas on how to find the financial security you desire. What is the financial story of your life? What chapter are you on? Just beginning? Are you halfway through? Creating the last chapters? If you could, would you like a chance to rewrite how your story has unfolded to date? Would you like to change the plotline? Or would you like to read ahead to see how the journey ends?

I can help you make your unwritten or unfinished story a more successful and less stressful journey. **In my view, the most important financial goal for most people is to find their way to financial security**. I am not talking about becoming a multimillionaire or better. I am not talking about the Financial Independence, Retire Early (FIRE) approach to your financial life, although I admire a lot of what the FIRE movement espouses. I am talking about living a relatively stress- and anxiety-free financial life. I am talking about knowing the key money decisions you will need to make and where to go to get help making them. I am talking about having the financial resources to draw on when they are needed. I can help get you there.

I was driven to write *The FinancialVerse* for several key reasons. The first is to provide a much-needed, big-picture financial overview of what a financial life should look like for the average person. I will do this using easily understood concepts and language. The second is to help people who live in what I call the "without world" to better understand what their financial lives should look like and what actions they can take to improve their lifelong financial journeys. Lastly, I want to give people guidance on why they should begin lifelong financial learning that will pay benefits many times over during their lifetimes. I don't believe we adequately prepare people for the financial decisions they will face in life. This book will help significantly with what you need to know regardless of where you are in your journey.

To help you, I am drawing on over thirty years' experience in the global financial services industry. I will offer you simple, proven ideas and practical advice to improve your financial life. I will make it worthwhile for you to read this book. It will help you reduce the anxiety and stress that financial matters can cause.

THE NEED FOR FINANCIAL EDUCATION

Despite a booming economy, record corporate profits, a healthy stock market, fifty-year low levels of unemployment, and improving wages, most people are struggling financially. They are one missed paycheck away from financial oblivion. The Center for Financial Services Innovation reported on November 1, 2018, in its inaugural *US Financial Health Pulse* (CFSInnovation.org) that only 28 percent of Americans can be considered financially healthy. This report struck home to me, as it summarizes what I have seen in my recent travels, reading, and experience in the financial services industry.

In an interview published in USA Today as part of the report's release, Jennifer Tescher, CEO of the Center for Financial Services Innovation, was quoted as saying: "We felt like we needed to create a definitive study that helped to demonstrate that while the larger economic headlines around a roaring stock market, and low unemployment, and great consumer spending are out there, that's not actually telling an accurate story."

The organization, which works with startups that are building financial health tools, surveyed more than five thousand Americans. Here are some of the report's key findings:

- Nearly half said their spending had equaled or exceeded their income in the last twelve months.

- Forty-four percent of those surveyed relied on credit cards to make ends meet.

- Only 45 percent have enough to cover three months of living expenses (even though the majority of Americans say they save whenever possible).

- Forty-two percent have no retirement savings.

- Thirty percent have more debt than is manageable.

The report aims to give a fuller picture of financial health than typical studies. "We tested dozens and dozens of indicators," Tescher was quoted as saying. Looking at something like annual income, for example, doesn't necessarily indicate whether someone can cover his or her expenses. "If you're not really understanding how people are managing their money in a day-to-day kind of way, you're missing the whole picture," she said.

As I write this introduction, I have seen the same financial reality that most Americans experience. My reading and research tell me the following about today's average American family's financial situation:

- About 80 percent of families live paycheck to paycheck.

- Over 60 percent of families would be in a financial panic if they needed to come up with $400 to cover an unexpected bill such as a medical cost, a major car repair, a house repair, or the unexpected costs of an accident.

- Consumer debt of all types is at historically high levels, with student loan debt increasing the fastest.

- The average family has less than $100,000 saved for their retirement, which will likely be twenty to thirty years in length.

- The average family has less than one month of their annual cash expenses in savings.

- A record number of individuals over age sixty-five are filing for bankruptcy protection.

Why are families struggling so much in favorable times? I believe the root cause is that we have not educated people about what to expect in their life's financial journey and what financial decisions they will be called on to make. They simply do not know what to do or where to go to get the help they need.

My belief is that families are in a much more precarious financial situation than the financial media is reporting. People are having great difficulty making their money stretch to meet all of their lifetime needs. As I have heard Philip Hudgins of InVida Financial Network say many times: "Most people run out of money before they run out of month."

Given today's economic environment, the pace of technological change, and projections of what our economy will look like over the next few decades, we are rapidly moving to a point where more and more families are approaching the financial abyss. It will not take much of a push to put them over the edge.

I strongly believe we have not properly prepared people of all ages about how money is earned, spent, saved, and invested. I am not talking about the realities of the frequently mentioned 1 percent or how to become a millionaire overnight. I am talking about attaining basic financial security for the majority of Americans regardless of which identity group, race, religion, or demographic cohort they identify with or belong to. The case for better education is abundantly clear from the financial distress most people face today. I know as my life progressed, I went from living in the "without world" to the reality of financial security and comfort I longed for. It's time we got back to common-sense basics because we have become detached from financial reality everywhere we look.

THE "WITHOUT WORLD"

I grew up in the "without world"—without sufficient food, reasonable clothing, financial resources, sufficient education, and practical knowledge of the social graces of life. I had no one to take me under his or her wing and educate me on how to live successfully. My role models came from generations of people who worked hard without educations and sufficient payback for their efforts. They continually lost out due to their lack of financial learning, which resulted in their inability to earn reasonable cash income and properly manage their money. They had to fight day-to-day to get the most meager of basics for their families. This cycle of wanting was passed from generation to generation.

To break this cycle, I had to learn the key aspects of living on my own. I needed to determine the lifestyle I wanted, how to earn enough income to support that lifestyle, what it meant to be educated, how to approach and manage my money, and how to deal with the practicalities of the outside world. Each day, week, and year was a major struggle. I lived in a constant state of without and feeling the anxiety of not knowing how I could get the financial resources I needed to succeed. I did not really understand the financial journey my life would take, as I was focused on just surviving in the short term. This "without world" has motivated me throughout my life. I made a vow to escape it and provide my family with financial security. In reality, my "without world" continued until I reached my thirties, when I clearly learned what I needed to do and how I wanted to live.

In my youth, like most people, I saw both my parents work as hard as they could to support our family with meager results. I respected them for all they did to support our family. They could not work enough hours to earn a livable income—similar to today's campaign to mandate a living hourly wage of fifteen dollars an hour for workers. My father worked seven days per week. In retrospect, he truly exemplified the concept of the working poor. He could not make enough money to get ahead regardless of the number of hours he worked. In fact, he never really got ahead in life—financially or in any other respect. He dealt with struggle after struggle—some were his fault, while others were created by happenstance. My mom saved us, as she had a part-time cleaning job at our neighborhood church that paid enough for our monthly groceries. There were many months that without her earnings, we would have had little to eat.

As I grew up, a good portion of my free time with my father, when he was not working, was spent collecting newspapers and scrap metal in our family truck during school nights (this was before recycling became a common practice). We would take what we collected to the scrap yard the next day after school when my dad got home from work to earn a few extra dollars to buy groceries. If he had a good week and we earned more money than expected, he would take me to the local bar, and I would sit with him and he would order me a birch-beer-flavored soda as he sipped his favorite cold brew fresh from the tap.

As the oldest of five children, I was really bothered by our financial situation. It seemed that everything I needed for school or play was a big ask. I could not join my friends for movies, parties, or other social events. This weighed heavily on me. I vowed at age eight (yes, age eight) and announced to the adults in my life that the "without world" would not be how I would live my life. It was simply too hard. I told my family members I would grow up to have a job that paid me well for my ideas and thoughts. I did not want to live as my parents did—paycheck to paycheck—hoping that something positive would come along to make our daily struggle easier.

From the time I was twelve on, I had to pay for my school clothes, spending money, and any other needs I had outside basic shelter, food, and medical care. (I later learned these were the toughest years for my mom and dad, as my father was underemployed for about five years and it was learned that my brother had major heart issues that needed medical attention—and we had no health insurance.) By providing for my own needs, including shopping for my school clothes at the local W.T. Grant, a now-bankrupt retailer which was located within walking distance from my home, I learned the importance and rewards of working. I mowed lawns, raked leaves, cleaned yards, and worked after school assisting the elementary school janitor to earn money. I worked my way through college as a campus tour guide, janitor at a local elementary school, and house painter.

The fruits of my labor were that I became the first person in my immediate family to graduate high school, graduate first in my class at college, join a profession, become a senior corporate executive and, in time, a multimillionaire. I ran several businesses, traveled the world, and met key business leaders, government officials, and celebrities.

I accomplished all this finding my own way. This was both good and bad. I made about every painful mistake you can in managing relationships and money, although I did not have to declare bankruptcy or experience foreclosure. I had no one to teach me what I should expect, what I should anticipate in life, and what life could and would financially throw at me.

My parents did teach me certain fundamental truths, however. From my father, I learned the importance of showing up on time and working hard. From my mother, I learned the importance of getting the best education I could and that without an education, I would be stuck in the "without world." My mother also instilled in me what would be the most valuable trait I would need to be successful in life—a positive, expectant attitude. I was to be positive regardless of how difficult things would get. If life threw lemons at me, I was told to make lemonade. There was no challenge I could not overcome. As such, I have lived most of my adult life on what my wife fondly calls the River Denial. Many times, I made things appear better than they actually were. Sometimes this was to my benefit and other times to my detriment.

Please know that I believe my parents did the best they could for me. Both of them only graduated eighth grade, were orphaned in their teens, and struggled mightily throughout their adult lives to support their family. They did not have solid role models or life coaches to help them through life's financial struggles. I was able to take care of my mother in the latter or Fulfilling Stage of her life (you will learn more about that in Chapter 5) such that she could live financially stress-free. My father died at what I believe to be a young age—sixty-eight, when I was thirty-four—and did not have the chance to enjoy my financial success. My parents gave me what knowledge they had about the world. It was not enough, however, to prepare me for the realities I would face.

Today in our society, we are taught history, math, science, religion, philosophy, the environment, politics, and gender issues. In my experience, however, we have not spent sufficient time learning how to run our lives financially, the key life events and risks we will face, the decisions we will need to make, the resources available to us, and the ramifications of poor decision making.

The difficulty in teaching people about their relationship with money is that each person's journey is decidedly different. Each person will make financial decisions based on their individual needs and desires. No two people will go through life and make a copycat set of decisions about what they will wear, how they will live, whom they will marry, how they will spend their free time, or how they will work. Each journey through what I call the FinancialVerse, although governed by the same set of ground rules and macroeconomic considerations, will differ in the decisions made and life experiences that will impact the traveler.

THE UPCOMING FINANCIAL ENVIRONMENT

It is of utmost importance for us to understand the major aspects of the financial world in which we live and function. As I write this book in early 2019, here are my thoughts on the major economic trends and challenges we all will face in the next few years:

- Our government is spending money at an unsustainable rate. Trillion-dollar deficits cannot continue and will require a resetting of our levels of taxation, spending, and the sacrosanct entitlement programs (e.g., Obamacare, Medicare, and Social Security) at some point in the near future.

- Social Security and Medicare retirement and Obamacare health benefits will need to be modified by Congress.

- Most adults alive today over the age of forty will work until they reach age seventy out of necessity. Only people who work jobs that require physical labor will retire at younger ages. I know that people plan and desire to retire in their early sixties, but this will become harder and harder to accomplish based on lower incomes from employment, lower retirement savings levels, and the increasing cost of health care in our later years.

- We are living longer, with most adults alive needing to plan to live into their mid- to late eighties at a minimum. Younger adults can expect to live into their nineties due to medical and technological advances. Those adults just reaching their twenties stand a good chance of living to be at least one hundred years old. Finding the cash to pay the basic bills for living longer will place an even greater stress on everyone.

- As a country, we have not fully planned for the costs of providing care to an ever-aging population. Most people believe, incorrectly, that Medicare will fully provide for the costs of caring for their aging and sick family members. In reality, Medicare does not pay for the costs of long-term care. The upcoming wave of people needing assistance for medical and cognitive problems is just starting. Neither our government nor our households have budgeted for the cost and lifestyle impacts of this aging wave of people.

- Young adults just entering the workforce will have an even greater number of jobs during their working lives than prior generations as we see the impacts of temporary or contract work and the gig economy.

- Unless a miracle happens and we have health care reform, basic medical costs will continue to increase at rates in excess of core inflation. We are reaching the point where most families cannot pay for the costs of health care even if they have health insurance due to large required coinsurance and deductible amounts. Our governmental leaders have been stuck in their partisan positions and have not focused on solving the problem of providing base health coverage—medical, psychological, dental, and vision—for the country.

- Employers are continuing to cut back on retirement and health benefits, providing minimal salary increases and not expanding benefits for the bulk of employees. While we hear about the inability of companies to find and hire the employees they need, we still have not seen the compensation increases necessary to attract these candidates.

- The basic costs of housing, food, education, and transportation continue to increase with inflation in at least the 2 to 3 percent range.

The above are the key financial challenges I believe we face. I am not trying to paint an overly negative environment. I just want to be realistic and not in a state of denial. Without a financially educated population, the probability of successfully dealing with the financial ramifications of the challenges each of us will face is not very good. We all have to get smarter in our financial decisions and the choices we make on a day-to-day basis.

I have written *The FinancialVerse* to provide the average person who is striving to succeed in this environment with an easy-to-read foundation to understand and better manage their financial journey in life. I want them to benefit from the mistakes I made, the experiences I had, and the knowledge I gained. **Having money is not the most important thing in life but having the right amount of money at the right time in life's journey is most important.** This is what financial security means to me. I want readers of this book to better understand the fundamentals of money and how they can use these fundamentals to have an anxiety-free, less stressful life for themselves and their families. I don't have all the answers, but I will provide you, the traveler, in the most jargon-free way I can, with an understandable foundation to improve and make your relationship with money more successful.

CHAPTER 1

THE FINANCIAL STAGES OF YOUR LIFE

I believe most people have three major stages to their financial lives: the Adulting, Striving, and Fulfilling Stages. Let me briefly explain each to you. Please be mindful that these stages apply for the vast majority of people. There are situations, however, where the suggested length of time in the stage will be more, or substantially less, than the suggested parameters I describe. An example would be if someone were able to generate a windfall of money through his or her productive efforts, an inheritance, or winning the lottery. They will move from what I call the Striving to the Fulfilling Stage of life. These types of events change the timing of the stages and can cause people to move from one stage to the other quickly.

Here are the three stages of your financial life in the FinancialVerse:

THE ADULTING STAGE

This stage takes place from birth to age thirty, when young people, in my view, are finally not their parents' responsibility. I also call this period The

Journey to Age Thirty. During this stage, the individual is educated, develops personal relationships such that they find a partner or friend group they affiliate with, finds steady employment or a career track to follow, and, lastly but most importantly, the individual is able to fully financially support themselves. To emphasize the last point, this would mean that the parents' bank closes on their thirtieth birthday unless a major emergency or unexpected need arises.

This period of thirty years is what many Baby Boomers will remember was either eighteen or twenty-one years for them. Many of you can still remember your parents saying that by the age of twenty-one, you needed to be out of the house and on your own. My dad kept telling me that by age eighteen, I was on my own. He said he had carried me as far as he could, and it was time for me to step up.

By the end of the Adulting Stage, the individual should emerge with a meaningful job and, most likely, student loan debt, which was used to finance a portion of their education. A distinct few will have accumulated sufficient savings—likely an emergency fund—and enough savings to afford a security deposit on a rental apartment or down payment on house. A very lucky few will have begun to save and invest for their Fulfilling Stage.

THE STRIVING STAGE

This stage takes place from ages thirty-one to seventy, resulting in a likely forty expected years of employment. During this period, today's young adults entering the workforce will likely have between ten and fifteen different jobs.

I know there is some controversy around increasing the age for ending full-time work to age seventy. I believe age seventy is the age most people will work to either as a result of projected changes in the retirement laws (e.g., Social Security and government retirement regulations) as well as the need for individuals to work longer to accumulate sufficient savings for the much longer life expectancy they will experience in the Fulfilling Stage.

The Striving Stage is the forty years the individual has to pay all their living expenses, pay for the cost of raising a family (if this is what they decide to do), and accumulate sufficient funds and income to provide for the Fulfilling Stage. You need to view these earning years as your key source of funds for your financial life unless you are the beneficiary of an inheritance or other windfall.

What are you going to do to make the most of these earning years? What approach do you want to take to balance work needs and personal needs? How hard are you willing to work? What jobs or fields of endeavor interest you such that you will want to spend forty years or a significant time period doing them? How do you educationally prepare yourself and your offspring for this long journey?

There are many questions to ponder, but the answers can and will differ for each individual. Lifelong learning will also be needed. After World War II, we sent people to college with the understanding that the education they received would last them for their working lives. Today, this is not the case. Too many changes take place in such a fast manner that the ability to learn new knowledge quickly is a skill each individual must master to be successful. The ability to continually learn new things is a skill we all need today.

By the end of the Striving Stage, the individual should have accumulated sufficient sources of funds and/or income streams to be able to fund their Fulfilling Stage. You will notice I do not use the word "retirement," as I believe it will become obsolete in a few years. If you are going to have a good chance to live to age one hundred, you will not want to play golf or sleep until noon from age seventy onward. Most people will want to do something meaningful with their time and physically will be able to do much more than prior generations of aging Americans.

Accumulation of resources for the Fulfilling Stage should include providing for the costs of whatever pleasure activities you want to pursue. This will include whatever charitable and/or community activities that are chosen. These costs would be combined with having sufficient health insurance and providing funds for unforeseen financial emergencies such as a major illness, long-term care protection, major house repairs, and the real risk that you will live much longer than you think possible. We will discuss understanding and providing for the costs of the Fulfilling Stage later.

THE FULFILLING STAGE

This is the post full-time working or Striving Stage of your financial life. This period is normally referred to as retirement, but I believe we need to rename this period of our lives to what it has become. That is a period of giving back by helping others along with the benefit of having the free time to do what pleases us most.

In my view, young adults today should plan for this stage to last from ages seventy-one to one hundred. For other demographic groups, particularly those over age sixty-five, they should plan to live until at least age ninety. As the nationally known financial expert Tom Hegna (TomHegna.com) has stated in his seminars, this stage has three discrete periods within it— the go-go years, the slow-go years, and lastly, the no-go years. Our collective hope is to not reach the no-go years for as long as possible. We will discuss these years in Chapter 5.

We all read much about this stage of life and the changing behaviors we are seeing. Today, most individuals are looking to use their later years to give back what they have learned or financially accumulated to their families and communities to make other people's lives better. They need time and financial resources to accomplish this. This book is part of my Fulfilling Stage, as I want others to learn from my life experiences as well as to benefit from my philanthropic actions. Giving money to causes or family members can be of great benefit and is relatively easy to do. You may, however, rather want others to benefit from your knowledge and life experiences. Your desire to return what you have been given to others will not happen without a plan.

For most people, the Fulfilling Stage also has some unfortunate aspects of aging associated with it. These include the impacts of increased health needs, possible cognitive decline, the complexities of income planning, and the possible impacts of estate-planning issues.

Each stage of your financial life has distinct questions, needs, and responsibilities. Each stage has its own key risks that must be addressed. You will need knowledge, coaching, and resources to successfully navigate each stage. Let's start your education by looking at the economic realities, the ground rules, and the key risks you find in the FinancialVerse.

CHAPTER 2

THE FINANCIALVERSE'S NEW ECONOMIC REALITIES, RULES, AND RISKS

THE ECONOMIC REALITIES OF 2019 AND BEYOND

If you are unaware, I would like to welcome you, your family, and your friends to the realities of the Fourth Industrial Revolution, which is just beginning. This revolution will reshape your relationship with technology, work, money, day-to-day activities, and relaxation. Don't know what this is or what the prior three revolutions were? You are not alone. Let me fill in the blanks for you.

THE FOUR INDUSTRIAL REVOLUTIONS

The First Industrial Revolution

This era began in Britain in the late eighteenth century and continued into the 1800s. In this time frame, the major change was that manufacturing moved from people's homes to powered factories. Production moved to larger-scale operations. This change saw factories powered by the innovations of using power generated by flowing water and steam to power industrial production as never before.

The Second Industrial Revolution

This era began around 1870 and continued to the start of World War I. This revolution was driven by the use of electricity, chemicals, and petroleum. Henry Ford and how he mastered the moving assembly line, creating great economies with mass production of goods, exemplified this era. The era is best known for the invention and harnessing of electric power to further drive production and supporting structures in daily life. Think of the time savings obtained by the invention of the automatic electronic washing machine versus hand washing of clothes.

The Third Industrial Revolution

This era began in the early 2000s and included the expansion of electronics and information technology to digitalize all aspects of how business and our personal lives are conducted. Think of the transition from the electronic manual typewriter to the word processor. We used to physically mail a letter, but today, we simply send an e-mail or text, which is received right away.

The Fourth Industrial Revolution

The Fourth Industrial Revolution is just beginning today and will go further than the third by combining physical, digital, and biological specialties to exponentially change all aspects of work and family life along with industrial production, management, where work is done, and corporate governance—with a related impact on our personal lives. Think of it as encompassing artificial intelligence (AI), robotics, the Internet of Things

(IOT), autonomous vehicles, 3-D printing, nanotechnology—the list goes on and on. How you work and live is about to be turned upside down.

As it unfolds, the Fourth Industrial Revolution will change the way we work, where we work, where we live, how we interact socially, and how we relax. Per authors such as Yuval Noah Harari, author of *21 Lessons for the 21st Century,* and Klaus Schwab, author of *The Fourth Industrial Revolution,* we should expect a transformation unlike anything we have seen in the past. Are you ready for this? Do you have the knowledge to be successful in this new world?

The reality for those working or preparing for their careers is that the Fourth Industrial Revolution will require them to learn new skills and acquire new knowledge throughout their working lives. Unfortunately, today, most students still attend educational institutions that teach and provide their service using the predominant post-World War II education model. The Fourth Industrial Revolution will dramatically change this. The demand for people who can think critically, work in teams, solve previously unsolvable problems, and apply new technologies will increase astronomically.

On the other side of this increase in demand for skilled workers, we will find that many of the lower-level, less-skilled jobs we are used to today (e.g., cashiers and clerical service positions) will be eliminated and the workers displaced. Think of this as the transition from your local convenience store to the new Amazon Go stores, we are beginning to see throughout the country. The Go stores are automated with customers able to purchase products with no cashier or self-checkout kiosk. This movement to cashier-less retail stores will increase dramatically as the technology used to implement this function is more widely available. In the World Economic Forum's recently released report titled "The Future of Jobs Report 2018," it was reported that we should expect that our economy will have a significantly number of current jobs eliminated as the technology rollout continues.

There is much debate as to whether new jobs will be created to deploy the displaced workers. My view is that so far, the new support jobs that have been created appear to offer less pay and benefits for the displaced workers. The new knowledge worker jobs this revolution is creating should enjoy higher wages and benefits, but there will be fewer workers to benefit from these jobs. This fourth revolution will create new societal issues that our government will need to address through a renegotiated social safety net, retraining programs, income subsidies, or other creative solutions. Income inequality will become more of an issue rather than less unless it is addressed.

The early impacts of this new revolution are starting to be seen in our economy as I write this book. These include increasing income inequality, a higher number of lower-paying jobs being created, and new business models emerging—think Uber, Lyft, Netflix, and, of course, Amazon.

Bottom line: the Fourth Industrial Revolution and its impacts will provide the key economic drivers for the future of the FinancialVerse, and you will need to understand them and how they impact the path you choose to follow to financial success. I am optimistic that new jobs will come forth to employ displaced workers, but the keys will be how long it will take for these jobs to emerge and the retraining individuals will need to take to qualify for these positions.

THE FINANCIALVERSE'S LANGUAGE

Like any state or country you visit, each destination has its own language and customs. The same is the case for the FinancialVerse. Just like you work to learn a few key words or phrases before taking that trip to a foreign country, you need to do the same as you prepare yourself for your financial journey.

Here are the key words and concepts you will most often come across in the financial media, advertising materials, and interactions in the FinancialVerse. They are easy to understand but require a little study to master. I can't stress enough that you need to understand these basic terms, or you won't understand the conversations that go on in the FinancialVerse. Here are the key terms and phrases you need to fully understand:

CASH FLOW – This is the essential foundation phrase. There is no progress in the FinancialVerse without positive cash flow.

It is an accounting term that simply means the cash you generate by working or investment and have available either in your pocket or in bank accounts. Positive cash flow means you are generating more cash than you are spending. Negative cash flow means you are spending more than you have coming in. Positive cash flow is the secret to success in the FinancialVerse.

BUDGET – A budget is a spreadsheet, financial application, or simple handwritten numerical listing of your expected sources of cash inflow and expenditures. Cash inflows come from your paycheck, child support payments, alimony received, and income from savings or investments. Cash outflows or expenses are what you pay for food, clothing, rent, mortgage, utilities, medical costs, entertainment, and other uses. Budgets are usually prepared for a period of at least six months to one year and show the amount of cash coming in, the cash going out, and the surplus or deficit that exists each period. When completing a budget, you can clearly see if your inflow of cash exceeds your expense outflow for bills.

Only about one-third of people actively set up and follow a budget. In my view, the two-thirds of people who do not have a budget in place ignore the reality of their financial situation and cast a blind eye to their money habits. This happens until the day they run out of cash or credit and an emergency has been created.

My advice is everyone needs a budget. Your goal in the FinancialVerse is to accumulate cash and, as such, your inflow has to exceed your outflow over time. If you constantly spend more cash than you earn, you are headed for financial failure.

EXPENSES – Expenses are the amounts you spend each day, week, and year to live. Expenses include the costs for housing, train fares, food, dining out, what you spend at Starbucks, student loan payments, car purchase or lease payments, Lyft costs, Uber costs, medical bills, clothing, entertainment, and other amounts spent.

You need to have a basic understanding of what you are spending for each type of item. You would be surprised how many people are totally blind to what they spend on a variety of things, in particular entertainment and clothing.

DEBT AND INTEREST EXPENSE – Debt is what you borrow from banks, family members, friends, and financial institutions and is usually evidenced by you signing a written agreement or note explaining how you will repay the debt and under what terms you have borrowed the money. Debt has many forms including credit cards, installment loans, student loans, mortgage loans, payday loans, and car loans. Each type of loan has different terms and costs. The cost for the debt you borrow is called interest expense. In addition to interest expense, you will sometimes give up an interest in the property acquired (e.g., mortgage and car loans) until the loan is repaid, agree to repay the loan over certain time frames (e.g., forty-eight months), sign different legal agreements, and pay different rates of interest expense depending on the loan type.

Interest expense varies based on the type of loan you use. The annual cost of the loan can range from single digits (e.g., 4 percent) for a mortgage to over 100 percent for payday loans. You need to understand the manner in which interest is charged on the loans you take out.

One way to understand the total cost of the money you are borrowing is to understand the annual percentage rate or APR of the loan. This percentage is required to be disclosed to you when taking out a loan based on state and federal Truth in Lending laws. The APR shows the full cost of the loan, including any fees you pay the lender to get the loan. It is the best way to make sure you have the real cost of the loan to understand and compare.

We will discuss various forms of debt in later chapters.

INTEREST INCOME – Interest income is the cash you earn from a bank or other financial institution from the deposits you have in your accounts. Interest income is earned based on the amount you have on deposit. It is calculated on a simple or compound basis. Interest is earned on the balance you have accumulated. If you continue to save and grow your balance on deposit, you will earn more interest. For example, your bank may pay you 2 percent annual interest on your savings account. If you have $10,000 on deposit, you will earn $200 per year in interest income. If you continue to save and have $20,000 on deposit, you would have earned $400 per year in interest income.

LIQUIDITY – Liquidity is the excess cash you have on hand or have access to in accounts you own. You access this liquidity to pay your bills or obligations. It is the amount you can withdraw right now or within a few days.

An example of liquidity is having an emergency fund available to pay for unexpected bills such as medical costs, parking tickets, or the need to travel to see a sick family member. In an ideal world, you should have at least six months of living expenses in your emergency fund at a minimum.

Everyone needs to be in a position where they have funds they can access in times of need. Liquidity applies to cash accounts, investments, and insurance products. Each will have rules as to how you can access any excess funds you have and the related costs to do so, if any.

THE RULE OF SEVENTY-TWO – This simple rule of finance is one you need to understand. Simply put, the rule number (i.e., seventy-two) is divided by the rate of interest you are earning for usually one year on your savings, and it will give you the number of years it will take for your investment to double in value. For example, if you are earning a consistent 6 percent on your investment, it will take you twelve years (seventy-two divided by six) to double your money. Another example would be if you were earning 2 percent annually on a savings account, it would take you thirty-six years to double your money.

Although there are equations and calculation methodologies available that are more precise, the rule of seventy-two is an easy-to-use way to calculate the magnitude of the return on an investment and its potential impact on accumulating cash. Learn how to apply it, and it can really improve your financial decisions.

ASSETS – An asset is a thing you own outright in your name. By owning it, you enjoy control over the asset and can do with it what you please. You can use it, destroy it, lend it to others, put it away for use in the future, share it with others, or sell it for cash or other valuable consideration. Over our lives, we buy and accumulate assets such as education, houses, cars, clothing, computer equipment, audio equipment, or other things.

What assets you acquire and how you decide to pay for them are two of the major decisions you will make in the FinancialVerse. For example, do you pay to purchase assets using cash, or do you borrow money to pay for them? Do you buy a new car, a used one, or would it be better to use Uber or Lyft to get you where you need to be?

LIABILITIES – Liabilities are obligations you owe for the costs of living and assets you purchase using debt. These include normal bills for food, housing, utilities, transportation, and eating out. They also include major items such as federal and state income and property taxes, real estate taxes, mortgage payments, and car purchase payments. Lastly, they also include payments you are legally mandated to make to others if you hurt them physically, mentally, financially, or economically.

Liabilities require you to pay cash to the person or entity to which you owe the money. You are usually required to pay liabilities by certain dates and times called due dates. Failure to pay your liabilities on time and in the correct amounts can result in financial penalties, the charging of interest expense and fees, or in certain situations the asset being taken from you by the person or institution to be sold to satisfy the obligation.

Protecting yourself against certain liabilities is important. Later, we will discuss ways you can conduct yourself and how to use available insurance products to eliminate or minimize the risk of having to make cash payments for certain liabilities.

BONDS – Bonds are obligations of companies that can be purchased for investment. There are numerous types, amounts, structures, and collateral backing bonds.

Individuals purchase bonds as an investment to earn interest income.

STOCK AND EQUITIES – Stock or equities represent fractional ownership in a company/corporation. For example, you might own ten shares of Apple Computer. People and businesses own stock because they want to share in the profits and value of the underlying business. Over time, it has been shown that returns to owners of stock can be the highest of any investment they can make.

There are numerous types or classes of stock. The ownership rights that each type of stock has are determined by the company issuing the instrument and by the federal and state laws that govern the creation and issuance of the shares.

MUTUAL FUNDS – A mutual fund is an investment consisting of different stocks or bonds. A mutual fund allows the owner to combine their money with others to make investments in companies. This often allows the mutual fund owner to use smaller amounts of investment dollars to make investments in many companies. This should reduce the risk to the owner of investing in individual companies and lessen risk by using the expertise of the mutual fund investment manager to oversee all investment decisions.

There are numerous types of mutual funds and hundreds of companies that sell mutual fund products. All products and product sellers are subject to significant federal and state regulation and oversight of their sales, marketing, and other business practices.

Mutual fund products can be purchased from mutual fund companies and have specific rules as to when they can be purchased, sold, and when they are taxed for federal and state income tax purposes.

CAPITAL GAINS AND LOSSES – A capital gain or loss is the profit or loss the owner receives from the sale of assets such as stocks, bonds, mutual funds, real estate, or other property. The gain or loss depends on what you receive for the sale of the capital asset compared to what you paid for it. There are numerous tax rulings and procedures on the definition of what a capital transaction is, if it is a gain or loss, when the gain or loss is taxed, and how to calculate the gain or loss.

If you have a capital gain or loss, you will likely need the expertise of a qualified tax accountant to assist you in determining how to report the transaction for income and other tax reporting purposes.

INDEX FUNDS AND ETFS – Index funds and exchange traded funds (ETFs) are mutual fund products that are traded like stocks on a stock exchange. These products can be bought and sold as quickly as the stocks that comprise them. For example, let's say you purchase a very popular Standard & Poor's 500 ETF. This ETF consists of shares of the five hundred companies that comprise the Standard & Poor's defined index. You can purchase and sell your shares at any time you can trade them. You control when the transactions take place and can determine the timing of when you pay tax on related capital gains or losses.

LIFE INSURANCE PRODUCTS – State-chartered and regulated life insurance companies issue life insurance products. The states regulate the companies and their ability to pay or solvency for all obligations for the products they sell.

I highlight life insurance products as an essential building block for your journey through the FinancialVerse because they are one of the few places you can go to buy guarantees that protect you against the key financial risks you will face.

For example, suppose you are married and have children. How do you protect your kids against the possibility that you die or become disabled unexpectedly and are unable to pay for the costs of their upbringing or college education? Maybe you are lucky enough to have savings that can cover this contingency. Most people do not. They instead purchase life insurance protection, which pays a lump sum upon their death that will provide the cash needed. This payment upon death is guaranteed if the premium payments for the policy are made and not claimed improperly (e.g., your family member took out a policy on your life and then killed you to collect the money).

A second great example of the power of guarantees in life insurance products is their use in retirement planning. Where can you go today to purchase guaranteed income that will last your entire life? The answer is to purchase an income annuity from a life insurance company that covers your life. The life insurance company guarantees to make the lifetime payments in exchange for the premium paid for the annuity. The life insurance companies can do this, as they insure large populations of people and can blend the risk.

THE TEN MUST-DOS

Here are what I believe to be the ten-basic must-dos or rules of the FinancialVerse. Following these rules will enable you to have a successful journey through the FinancialVerse. Please look at and try to fully comprehend each, as they are critically important:

1. Spend two hours per week understanding and keeping up to date with the FinancialVerse. This means you will need to read, listen to, or watch media to understand current leading financial indicators, economic developments, key financial terms and concepts, and basic financial math. Much will change as new technologies are introduced and implemented. Keep informed of these changes.

2. Have a budget or ongoing record of cash coming in and going out. I learned early in my career that what is not measured is not managed. You can't navigate your journey if you don't know how you are doing and where you are going. In the FinancialVerse, this is done by understanding and managing your inflow and outflow of cash. Think of yourself as a plumber. You are trying to make sure your water pipe flowing cash is used as needed and does not have holes in it, leaking without your knowledge.

3. Using crowd-funding sources such as GoFundMe to raise emergency cash is not a reliable financial backup strategy. I can't stress this enough in what I see each day. Recently, I knew of the death of a man in his twenties in a car accident. His obituary showed the Internet address where contributions could be made to take care of his family and funeral costs.

   You must become financially self-reliant. You must protect your income, assets, and family. You cannot depend on the kindness of others to bail you out of difficult circumstances. These people may not be there when you need them, and your dependents may suffer as a result.

4. Understand the new ways to acquire and pay for things you need to live in our economy today. There are five major ways to get the use of things you need—buy them for your exclusive use, rent them for your exclusive use, barter for them, subscribe to use them sharing with others for a fee, or, lastly, get them for free in exchange for your personal data or service (think Google and Facebook). Each of these ways has positives and negatives. Where

you are in your financial life and your personal values will determine which action you take to acquire the things you need to live. For example, you may want to own your home rather than rent or live with others. You may decide to do this because you want the privacy and peace of mind in completely controlling your living arrangements.

5. Debt can be your friend if you understand how to use and not abuse it. We will discuss the types of debt and how to use them later in this book. The major caveat here is you should only use debt if you can afford it and can comfortably repay the obligation.

6. There are certain financial risks you must identify, eliminate, or minimize. I have identified eight key financial risks that can negatively impact your journey through the FinancialVerse. I will review each of them with you and provide some ideas on how to eliminate or minimize their potential negative impact on your journey.

7. Time is an advantage you must utilize. The sooner you take charge of your journey through the FinancialVerse, the sooner you will progress. Time is your friend when you are young and can be your enemy if you are older. You can't get the years back. Remember the saying, "You can't make a baby in one month with nine women." Certain financial things in life take time; they cannot be overcome with last-minute actions.

Here is a quick example of the importance of taking advantage of time. Let's say you want to start saving for the older years of your life when you are not working full time. You have two options—begin saving $10,000 each year on your birthday in a lump sum at age twenty-two or wait until age thirty-two to start the program. Let's assume you can earn 7 percent on your money through a combination of stocks and bonds. Let's see what this looks like.

Here is what you would accumulate if you started saving at age twenty-two at a 7 percent return:

Age	Total Accumulated Savings
22	$10,000
25	$44,399
55	$1,282,588
60	$1,856,403
65	$2,661,209

Here is what you would accumulate if you started saving at age thirty-two at a 7 percent return:

Age	Total Accumulated Savings
22	$0
25	$0
32	$10,000
35	$44,399
55	$581,767
60	$873,465
65	$1,282,588

By starting ten years earlier, you would have accumulated $1,378,621 more. That is the difference between the amounts of $2,661,209 for age twenty-two and $1,282,588 for age thirty-two. The delay results in you having almost half as much in accumulated savings to fund the later years of your life. This simple example shows the impact of starting a disciplined savings approach early in your financial life and the power of compound interest income.

8. Know the gatekeepers who can derail your progress. As in life, having good financial role models and knowledgeable coaches can markedly improve the success of your journey. In the FinancialVerse, there are a number of resources available to you that you should avail yourself. Most people do not use these resources. There are also entities that can have a positive and negative impact on your journey such as banks, credit rating agencies, insurance companies, and other financial institutions.

9. Starting over or hitting the reset button during your journey through the FinancialVerse can be costly and can have major negative effects on your travels. Hitting the reset button in the FinancialVerse usually means filing for one or more types of bankruptcy. There are positive and negative aspects of bankruptcy that must be thoroughly understood. We will address these shortly.

10. Look for guides or coaches to help you navigate and succeed. Contrary to what you often read in the financial press, there are different types of qualified people in the FinancialVerse that can help you get where you need to be. Who they are and whom you should consult will depend on where you are with your journey and what problem you are trying to solve. I will try to point out key resources you should look to consult for advice.

THE EIGHT KEY RISKS

To guide your journey through the FinancialVerse, you must explicitly consider the financial risks you will face and how you can eliminate or mitigate each. These risks can be easily understood and will seem second nature to you, but they must be explicitly addressed by you—the traveler. If not, you may encounter major detours, potholes, and challenges to your financial life. A key learning is to know there are ways each of these risks can be dealt with. It just takes a little time and effort on the part of the traveler. In my view, it is essential for you to address each risk.

Based on my experience, here are the key financial risks in the FinancialVerse that you will encounter:

- Education Risk – The risk of obtaining too much or too little education, or pursuing a trade, concentration, or profession that will not qualify you to earn reasonable cash income.

- Cash Income Shortfall Risk – The risk of not earning sufficient cash income to support your needs.

- Disability Risk – The risk of becoming physically or mentally disabled and not able to continue to work.

- Health Risk – The risk of becoming ill and not having sufficient resources to pay for the costs of care. This risk includes providing for the cost of long-term care during the Fulfilling Stage should you need it. The long-term care need is the risk elephant in the room as far as I am concerned.

- Premature Death – The risk of dying too young and not being able to earn the income and accumulate the assets necessary to support your needs or leave funds to provide for the future needs of your dependents. In the famous Motown song sung by The Temptations, "Papa Was a Rollin' Stone," the lyrics went something like: "Papa was a rollin' stone. And when he died, all he left us was alone." Be it a man or a woman, dying too soon and not leaving cash for your dependents is not what you want to do.

- Debt Risk – The risk of accumulating or relying on too much or too costly debt such that the debt cannot be comfortably repaid from current cash income.

- Liability Risk – The risk that you will physically, emotionally, professionally, or financially harm someone in an accident in your car, home, or other physical or digital location and be held legally responsible to pay cash damages to the person you harmed.

- Longevity Risk – The risk that you live a very long life and won't have the cash income to pay your living expenses. It is the risk of running out of money in old age when you are unable to work. The risk of running out of money in old age is a major concern in our society today.

We will discuss each of these risks in this book and present possible ways you can eliminate or mitigate the impact of each.

As you design your journey through the stages of the FinancialVerse, plan on addressing these risks using your own financial resources and by the decisions you make. How you approach and solve each risk is a function of your individual circumstances. For example, if you decide to have children, you will take on the added responsibility to provide for them until they can provide for themselves. If you don't have children, you will not have to plan on how to fund these costs. Or if by chance you hit the genetic jackpot and inherit poor physical health genes, you will need to plan to have your health risk and related expenses properly covered.

CHAPTER 3

THE ADULTING STAGE — THE JOURNEY TO AGE THIRTY

I can still remember my father telling me to be fully prepared to financially support myself by the time I turned eighteen and graduated high school. He told me very clearly that he was done carrying me. He did not have a high school education and felt he had given me more than he got in life. These words of advice were preceded by a conversation we had when I was twelve when he told me if I needed school clothes, I should plan to work to pay for them. He could not afford to buy them for me. After this, I began my work life by mowing lawns and doing yard work—the first of many side gigs. By me reaching these ages, he had fulfilled some or all of his parental responsibilities to me. He had given me the best he could muster. Baby Boomers reading this book will likely remember a similar talk from their parents.

Given today's longer life spans, the need to obtain higher levels of education, our changed parenting styles, and current economic trends, I believe this date of financial independence has been extended from age eighteen to age thirty. In reality, we have extended adolescence, pushing the adoption of adult behaviors, including reaching financial independence, to later and later in life. This period from birth to adult independence is the Adulting Stage of the FinancialVerse or the Journey to Age Thirty, as I refer to it.

In this first thirty years of life, we should complete our general education about how the world works; have the key experiences of growing up; make our first social, professional, business, and personal relationships; learn how to learn; and develop our emotional footprint or what many call our emotional foundation. During this stage, we educate ourselves such that we can function as productive citizens in society. Given today's financial world, by age thirty, we should have obtained the knowledge to effectively navigate the world and to be able to generate sufficient cash income to support ourselves.

During this journey, our primary and secondary public and private schools provide a full curriculum of subjects covering math, science, and the liberal arts. In my opinion, what we don't teach is a practical understanding of the FinancialVerse, including the financial risks we will face in our lives and the knowledge foundation of financial topics that are needed to be successful. This foundation should be such that we enable the student to pursue a trade or field of knowledge that qualifies them for a job that will produce an inflow of cash sufficient to support them in the lifestyle they choose and provide the skills needed to make the decisions necessary to mitigate the financial risks they will face.

If the student acquires knowledge in areas that are not commercially needed in our economy, they are taking the first step toward failure in the FinancialVerse. If the skills needed to generate a cash income aren't obtained, there is no way the individuals will be able to create a reasonable lifestyle. I can't stress enough that without developing a commercially viable skillset, the individual will be forced by the FinancialVerse into a day-to-day struggle to make ends meet with even the most minor financial decisions, causing consternation and anxiety and creating possible conflict in their lives. I am not being cold about pursuing learning for learning's sake but am presenting the reality of our economy. Our society is not yet structured to provide a basic income stipend or subsidy to individuals to provide for the pursuit of personal desires. The cold reality is that if you don't have employable skills, you will suffer throughout your life.

THE COSTS OF LEARNING

As with any endeavor that is worthwhile, learning takes time, money, and dedication to be successful. For most of us, we are not born into families that have the financial resources to fully fund all thirty years of our Adulting Stage. To our benefit, we are all beneficiaries of free, publicly funded elementary and secondary education, but if we decide to gain the knowledge to pursue a trade or profession, we will need to find the money to pay for that education. As reported on the website Student Loan Hero (StudentLoanHero.com) on February 4, 2019, we have now accumulated over $1.5 trillion of student loan debt to finance our post-secondary school educations. For many people, the significant amount of student loan debt they have accumulated will not pay off in a future income stream and will saddle them with a crushing monthly debt load they can't get out from under for most of their earning years. Based on a recent Research Issue Brief titled "Student Loan Debt Trends and Employer Programs to Help," published in December 2018 by the Employee Benefit Research Institute (EBRI.org), the people suffering most with the burden of debt are those who do not ultimately finish their college education and attendees at for-profit institutions.

As a society, we have not given enough thought and information about the economic value of higher education. For the most part, we have directed most everyone down a path to obtaining a college education that would assure them of a high-paying job and a great start to their Striving Stage.

Unfortunately, one must choose a field of learning very carefully. With the average four-year college education costing between $38,000 at an in-state public college or university to over $140,000 at private institutions, how this decision is made couldn't be more important. Choose a trade or profession that is not in demand, and you have wasted time, money, and work that will not pay off for you. As an added impact for many students, they will have the pleasure of repaying student loans for a good portion of their adult lives.

To be successful in the Adulting Stage, obtain a careful mix of formal and practical learning for yourself or your children. This mix will be different from the post-World War II model of education most Americans have experienced. The cost benefit tradeoffs obtaining this education need to be carefully weighed and openly discussed within the family.

As mentioned above, the costs of post-secondary learning range between $38,000 and $140,000 for an undergraduate degree. There are benefits to a properly chosen college education that include:

- You should earn more money during your lifetime. According to a recent post on CollegeBoard.org, the typical bachelor's degree recipient can expect to earn 66 percent more than a high school or secondary school graduate.

- Better jobs usually provide better benefits, including life, health, disability, and retirement. These benefits should enable you to address and mitigate some of the FinancialVerse's key financial risks.

- Having a profession should provide you with increased opportunities to obtain even better, higher-earning jobs.

- To make the learning decision, you will need to balance what I call the Education Equilibrium Scale of the desire to learn a subject and its potential to provide future income for you. The best education is the one that balances your interest in pursuing an area with the probability of the future income it provides. For example, becoming a medical doctor will likely provide significant future income. However, if you cannot stand the sight of blood, you will not enjoy the profession. Ultimately, the trade-off for all of us is to choose an area of knowledge (e.g., technology, science, computing, marketing, management) that we enjoy and have a passion for that is in demand by employers and can produce a reasonable level of future income that will provide for our future needs in the FinancialVerse.

STUDENT LOAN DEBT – FRIEND OR FOE?

As I write this in early 2019, US student loan debt has reached over $1.5 trillion. According to the Employee Benefit Research Institute Research

Issue Brief titled "Student Loan Debt: Trends and Implications" dated July 9, 2018, the share of families with student loan debt has increased from 10.5 percent in 1992 to 22.3 percent in 2016. The median amount owed by each family has risen from $5,363 in 1992 to $19,000 in 2016.

The reasons for the increase in this type of debt are the increased cost of a tertiary education, inflation in higher education costs, and falling incomes from the global recession of 2008, which reduced family savings put aside to help pay for college costs. As noted in the EBRI's issue brief, the median monthly payment for this debt was about $200 per month in 2016. This required monthly payment places a burden on family budgets and places significant pressure on the ability to make purchases of other needed items such as a home and living expenses.

The keys to using student loan debt are to minimize what is taken out and only incur this debt to fund a learning or education that will produce a viable future cash income stream. I can't stress this enough. Look to get the maximum valuable education at the lowest loan amount. Buying the best college education you can afford is the key. Not the most prestigious. The lesson we are seeing play out today is that as a student, don't take on loans unless you are clearly focused on the education you are investing in and its potential future payback. Attending a prestigious college or university to study a field of knowledge for which you cannot get a job is a costly decision only a few very well-off students can make.

For most people, taking on debt to finance learning that is nice to have will have major lifetime negative impacts on their journey through the FinancialVerse. Think of it this way—having to pay an extra $500 per month in loan repayments for fifteen years means you will need to earn or designate for debt service an additional $120,000 in income (at a 25 per-cent effective income tax rate) over that period of time or $8,000 per year.

We are seeing families and individual students take different actions to reduce loan amounts by using new strategies. Here are several I have seen:

1. Actively talking about college costs and how to pay for them. This includes acknowledging the impact of the cost of the higher education on the future spending, retirement, savings, and cash flow of the family and the student.

2. Requiring that the student have financial skin in the game with respect to their education by using their own cash to pay for a portion of classes and costs. If a student has to directly pay for a portion of their education, they will think twice about what they are spending.

3. Attending a lower-cost local community college for the first two years of college, then transferring to a major institution to complete the degree.

4. Attending a local college or university system within the state where they are a resident, to take advantage of lower in-state tuition rather than attending a costlier private or out-of-state public institution.

5. Having the student take a year off after graduation or what is called a "gap year," which is so evident outside the United States, to either work or travel to find out what they really want to do.

By doing this, the student will be able to enroll in tertiary schooling firmly understanding the field they want to study and with an additional year of maturity.

In obtaining a student loan, there are two major types of lenders—the federal government and private sources.

> ➢ The federal government guarantees federal loans. They come with some benefits that may not be offered by private lenders, including income-driven repayment options, loan forgiveness programs, and fixed interest rates. Plus, some federal loans are subsidized, which means the government will foot the bill for the interest on the loan while the student is in school.

> ➢ Private loans come from banks, credit unions, or schools. In some cases, nonprofit agencies provide a guarantee for student loans, or lenders may self-insure. A private loan may have a variable interest rate, which means the interest rate you pay can change.

As you can see, there are many ways to get the resources needed to finance the learning needed to succeed in the FinancialVerse without overextending the student in debt. To accomplish this, careful planning is needed.

FINANCIAL GATEKEEPERS

In the FinancialVerse, there are organizations that track and monitor how you manage your money, in particular how you use and pay back any credit borrowings (e.g., credit cards, retail cards, and personal loans) or ongoing obligations (e.g., utility and medical bills) for which you are responsible. I call these organizations the financial gatekeepers. Here is a brief summary of the key financial gatekeepers you will encounter.

CREDIT REPORTING AGENCIES – As you journey through the FinancialVerse, the results of your financial credit decisions will be closely monitored by what are called credit reporting agencies. The credit reporting agencies are the key gatekeeper for you to obtain the credit you need during your lifetime. The three main agencies are Equifax, Experian, and TransUnion.

These agencies monitor key aspects of the credit relationships you establish. They mainly look at five key aspects of your actions, which include:

1. Your payment history

2. Credit utilization

3. Credit age – how long the relationships have been in place

4. Recent credit applications

5. Mix of credit

Each of the credit reporting agencies has extensive websites that describe their ratings and the process conducted to determine them. The websites will also direct you as to how to correct any information that is incorrect in the final reports. Your bank or credit card company usually has a section of their website that shows your credit scores.

The agencies each have a scoring system for this information. The majority based their ratings on what is called a FICO score. The FICO score is a system developed by Fair Isaac Corporation dating back to 1958. There are twenty-eight different FICO scores that are used to analyze various types of creditworthiness. The most common score, however, that is used by the credit agencies is your FICO 8 score. This score, which is given on a sliding scale of 300 to 850, determines your creditworthiness. A score of 780 and above puts you in the highest category while a score below 600 puts you in the bottom rung. The higher your rating, the lower the cost of the credit you are seeking and the more likely you are to secure the financing you seek. Entities looking to extend credit to you will usually access your information from one or all of the credit reporting agencies as part of the credit granting process. They will use this information along with their own proprietary analysis in granting credit.

For the full information on your credit score, how it is determined, and how you should monitor your scores, please visit MyFICO.com. You can also get background information on your scores from the websites of the three main agencies. The FICO scoring system is updated periodically. For example, in 2019, the FICO 9 score is being introduced. This new score will take into consideration how consumers manage their cash in checking, savings, and money market accounts with the objective of granting higher scores to lower-rated individuals who manage their affairs better than others. The new score will also look at medical debt, paid collections, and rental history different than other scoring systems.

Your credit score is calculated from the first time you incur an obligation for a service such as a utility, medical bill, or Internet subscription. The majority of companies to whom you are paying the obligation report the timeliness of your payments to the credit reporting agencies and create a permanent record of your actions. It is one of the key determinants of your ability to get credit. You must know your score and monitor it.

BANKS AND OTHER FINANCIAL INSTITUTIONS – In addition to credit reporting agencies, other financial institutions that can either help or negatively impact your journey are banks, insurance companies, finance companies, department stores, retail stores, and technology providers. Each of these usually takes selected FICO scores and adds their own proprietary credit analysis to determine if they will extend credit or coverage to you.

Overall, my advice is to be responsible in your financial dealings—pay your bills on time. Fully comply with all credit application requests for information. Do not enter agreements to purchase goods and services that you do not understand. Be vigilant at all times when it comes to your credit.

WHAT IF I FAIL IN MY JOURNEY?

In the FinancialVerse, your journey may fail, and you may run out of cash and be unable to pay your bills and living costs. You may be unable to earn the cash income you need to support the lifestyle you want. You may lose your job and be unable to pay your bills. You may become sick and disabled and deplete your savings. These possible events will cause you to make choices and shape your journey through the FinancialVerse to live a reasonable lifestyle on what income you have. You may also unexpectedly take on more financial responsibilities than you can handle, or one of the key risks—like the costs of caring for a sick relative—may force you off your path or overwhelm you.

There are ways to get out from under such a crushing and unexpected financial burden, but the release from these obligations comes at a cost. Typically, each state has laws that allow individuals who have been unable to manage their financial affairs to get a fresh start or, as the laws state, to reorganize their finances. These options are typically written into law at the state and national levels.

Most often, the quickest fail or reset button that is hit by persons in financial trouble to provide relief is reorganizing the individual's financial situation by filing for court-ordered bankruptcy protection. Bankruptcy protection allows you time to get your affairs in order, negotiate with creditors, and try to work out a plan that will let you reset your financial life. There are two common types of individual bankruptcy protection: Chapter 7 and 13 bankruptcy filings. Should you need to reset your financial circumstances, you need to understand the ramifications of all options. My advice is to consult a bankruptcy attorney. The attorney can advise you on the steps you need to take and will explain the ramifications of the bankruptcy filing.

There are costs to file bankruptcy and major implications for you. Here are some considerations:

> ➢ Filing bankruptcy does not legally discharge certain types of debt. These usually include student loan debt, court-ordered child support obligations, court-ordered alimony, and most tax debts.

> Filing bankruptcy can relieve financial stress from bill collectors, help stabilize your cash flow so you can regroup, and allow you to get your affairs in better order for the future in a timelier manner.

> There are costs to file including those charged by attorneys and the courts.

> If the debt being discharged in bankruptcy is secured (e.g., a car loan or mortgage/home equity), the lender can take possession of the asset—the car or house—to sell the asset to help pay back the loan.

> Lastly, having a bankruptcy filing will stay on your credit record and impact your credit score—seven years for a Chapter 13 filing and ten years for a Chapter 7—usually having a negative impact on your ability to get credit in the future if you need it. Consult the websites of the three main credit-reporting agencies for how each handles a bankruptcy filing.

Overall, hitting the reset button with a bankruptcy filing should only be done after careful thought, negotiations with your creditors, and consultation with a bankruptcy attorney. Filing can have lasting impacts on your ability to access credit at times when you may need it most as you restart your financial life, including purchasing or renting a residence, buying or leasing a car, or obtaining financing for another major purchase.

STAGE SUMMARY

The journey to age 30 or the Adulting Stage of the FinancialVerse should prepare you for life's journey. You should emerge from this stage with:

> ➤ The ability to learn how to learn. This will prepare you for what is an ever-changing world where you are called on to learn new skills to adapt to technological innovations.

> ➤ Student loan debt that has been carefully acquired and used to pay for an education that will produce employable skills.

> ➤ An education and experiences that enable you to earn a cash income sufficient to support yourself and your family, if you have chosen to start one.

> ➤ An understanding that your financial decisions are increasingly monitored by third parties who will rate you on how well you have managed your financial obligations.

> ➤ A realization that if you fail in managing your financial life, there are ways to reorganize your affairs that come with what can be heavy costs.

CHAPTER 4

THE STRIVING STAGE (AGES THIRTY-ONE TO SEVENTY)

FORTY YEARS TO CREATE INCOME AND ACCUMULATE ASSETS

The Striving Stage is the forty-year period from roughly age thirty-one to age seventy that you have to earn income to pay your current living expenses and accumulate assets for the Fulfilling Stage. For those of you who are young adults, this will likely translate into working for ten to fifteen different employers over your careers. If you look back, your parents and grandparents were likely to work for four to six employers for all their earning years.

THE NEW TYPES OF WORK

The definition of work has changed in recent years and will continue to evolve as we enter the Fourth Industrial Revolution. Today, in my opinion, there are three major types of work/income-producing activities—full-time jobs (defined as thirty hours or more per week), part-time jobs (defined as fewer than thirty hours per week), and, lastly, the contracting or gig economy where people are paid based on completing a specific project, task, or service. In recent years, we have also seen that people are earning substantial money by collecting cash for sharing their owned property or selling personal possessions such as their data. This passive activity, while not formally acknowledged as work, is continuing to grow.

Each of the above types of employment comes with different pay arrangements, non-cash compensation, and psychological impacts. Securing full-time employment is usually the most financially beneficial in all aspects, but part-time work or performing side gigs may provide more lifestyle flexibility in exchange for lower financial compensation. Part-time jobs may also create a less anxiety-filled life over the commitments of a full-time position.

Regardless of the type of work you pursue, there are practical considerations you need to learn and address in your Striving Stage. Let's look at the major items.

THE COSTS OF LIVING

What does it cost you to live? How much do people spend to live each year? Is there a baseline amount you need to live? These are questions people ask as they begin to really look at what they spend each year and how it compares to other people. Luckily, there are reference sources you can consult. The most sourced reference is the federal government's Bureau of Labor Statistics (BLS) (bls.gov). Each year, BLS publishes a survey of data on consumer expenditures, income, and other demographic information. This comprehensive survey defines a consumer unit as a household with either a single person or two or more people living together who make joint financial decisions.

According to the BLS's April 26, 2018, Consumer Expenditure Survey covering the year 2016, the average American household earns $74,664 and spends about $58,460 per year for shelter, food, clothing, entertainment, insurance, and other necessary items. Please take some time to read the full survey at bls.gov should you have trouble sleeping.

The survey breaks down what the average consumer unit spends in a year as follows:

Food	$7,407
Housing	$19,325
Apparel and services	$1,771
Transportation	$9,252
Health care	$4,710
Entertainment	$2,941
Education	$1,372
Cash charitable contributions	$2,088
Personal insurance and pensions	$6,938
Other	$2,656
Total	**$58,460**

I think this information is great to use to compare what you and your family spend each year. Naturally, this amount can range either lower or higher depending on where you live. For example, a family living in New York City may spend substantially more to live compared to someone living in the outskirts of Atlanta, Georgia. I think it is a great idea to show this information to your teenagers to help with their financial education. It can help introduce the reality of financial life to them.

What you spend to support your lifestyle is a key decision you make. Must you have the most stylish clothing? Should you purchase a new car every four years? Must you eat out several times per week? Do you need to attend all the latest movies, shows, and sporting events? Do you need to have all the available streaming services, or can you get by with just one?

If these are your choices, the end result is that your lifestyle will be much more expensive than someone who displays much more frugal habits such as keeping their car for twelve years, not owning a car and using Lyft or Uber, not dining out, or carefully maintaining an attractive but less stylish wardrobe. The lifestyle decisions are yours, and they do differ significantly from person to person.

The costs of your lifestyle determine your basic cash outflow needs in the FinancialVerse. As I have said, these needs differ for each individual and are based on their daily decisions as to what is important.

CREATING AND MAINTAINING A BUDGET

As I have mentioned earlier, one of the key rules of the FinancialVerse is that you must keep track of what cash you earn, spend, and save. You do this by using a budget. A budget can range from a simple written list of your cash inflow and outflow items to the use of detailed and sophisticated computer applications. If you don't already have a budget, I think it is a great idea to go through this exercise in an old-school way—with a pencil and paper. This will force you to see each item of income and expense and make clear what you are earning and spending. Once you have created this awareness, you can move to one of the available personal budgeting applications that are available for your home computer, smartphone, or tablet.

Some great personal budgeting apps I have seen recently recommended include:

- Acorns
- Clarity Money
- CountAbout
- Expense Keep
- Expenses OK
- EveryDollar
- Goodbudget
- Mint
- PocketGuard
- Quicken
- YouNeedABudget (YNAB)
- Wally

Each of the above budgeting applications has pluses and minuses about how they operate. Please do a search to find and read the technology reviews for each and determine which application is best for you. Some of these applications are available from the Apple and Android app stores, but others must be purchased directly from the company. Finding a budgeting application that best meets your needs will make the budgeting process much easier for you.

Remember that in the FinancialVerse, you need to know where you are on your journey at all times. The only way to do that is to track your progress and measure success on a frequent basis. It takes time to get properly set up, but the ongoing benefits in planning and controlling your journey with money are substantial.

ESTABLISHING BANK ACCOUNTS – CHECKING, DEBIT, AND CREDIT CARDS

A major step as you begin the Striving Stage is to establish a relationship with a bank. As part of this relationship, you will need to set up a checking account, set up a savings account, obtain a debit card, and, if you qualify, obtain a credit card.

A checking account is an account you will use to pay the majority of your bills each month, deposit your paycheck, and use for debit card transactions. A debit card is a card that will allow you to make payments and pay for goods or services directly from your bank account. These payments are withdrawn from your account as they are made. A credit card allows you to pay for goods and services but with the option to repay them over time. This option comes with a cost, as the bank will charge you interest (sometimes as high as 36 percent) for the amounts not repaid on time. This option allows you to buy things you can't pay for fully, but at a very high cost.

To minimize the costs and fees you pay for banking services, look to online banks for the best deal. Without the need to support a brick-and-mortar branch network, they can offer you better terms and rates on your banking needs.

OBTAINING THE USE OF ASSETS AND SERVICES

In today's FinancialVerse, there are five major ways to obtain assets, products, and services. Let's look at each of the options available to you:

1. **BUYING** the asset, product, or service for your <u>exclusive use.</u> For example, this would be the direct purchase of a car or bicycle. You own 100 percent of the item purchased, and you can do with it what you want. It is legally yours in all respects. You can use it as you wish, sell it, or throw it away without any restrictions placed on you.

2. **RENTING OR LEASING** the asset, product, or service for your <u>exclusive use</u> in exchange for a rental or leasing payment. For example, this would include renting a car or bicycle on a daily basis or longer period. Rental terms, conditions, and restrictions are usually evidenced by a legal contract called a lease. In this case, you rent 100 percent of the use of the item, but there are restrictions on what you can do with the item because you do not legally own it. It is yours to use during the rental period, but there are restrictions on the use including you cannot sell the item to another party or damage the item without paying for the repair, as you do not own it.

3. **BARTERING** by trading an asset you fully own or a service you provide in exchange for a different item or other service. For example, you could trade your 1992 Ford truck for a 1999 Chevy truck if the other party agreed to the trade. Or you could barter by trading twenty hours of your service as a landscaper for catering services for your child's birthday party.

4. **SUBSCRIBING** to use an asset, product, or service. As a subscriber, you <u>share use</u> of the item with other subscribers for a fee that is substantially less than the cost of buying or renting the item for your exclusive use. An example would be subscribing to view a selection of music (Pandora) or movies/TV shows (Netflix or Hulu) for a monthly fee. You get use or enjoyment of the item for a limited period, but there are restrictions on what you can do with it because you do not legally own the item or have long-term exclusive use. The item or service is yours to use in limited respects during the period of the subscription.

5. **GETTING FREE USE** of the asset, product, or service in exchange for the access/use of your personal data or service labor by the offering service. Think Facebook, Twitter, Google, and other similar services. You get limited exclusive use of the product or service but allow the provider to use the data from your search, spending, reading, or enumerable other personal actions to sell to organizations that are looking to sell you products. While this is the least out-of-pocket way to secure the use of products and services, you may be compromising your personal confidential information with unknown third parties.

So, which of the five ways is best? You will not like my answer, as it depends. Renting a house may provide the best economic outcome to you. You may, however, feel more psychologically secure owning your own home and having exclusive use and control of it. The key in today's FinancialVerse is knowing there are different ways to get the use of an asset, product, or service and choosing the way that is best for you at the time.

PROTECTING YOUR GREATEST ASSET – YOUR INCOME

Once you have entered the Striving Stage, your most significant financial asset will likely be your ability to earn cash income by working in your chosen field, trade, or profession. But suppose just after completing the education or training you wanted and starting your dream job, you are struck down by a debilitating illness or a major accident. This is not your fault, but life crises happen in the FinancialVerse.

What happens to the future income you planned on earning? What happens to your savings plan for the Fulfilling Stage of your life? How do you provide for your family if this happens? How do you recover your investment in the education or training you obtained in the Adulting Stage? How do you protect against this risk? According to information compiled by the American Academy of Family Physicians (AAFPIns.com), approximately 35 percent of working individuals will have an event that will make them disabled for some period of time. The answer to these questions lies in government programs and purchasing private disability income insurance.

If you are unfortunate and become disabled and unable to work, the federal and state governments have programs that can help you if you qualify.

These programs include Social Security disability and state workers' compensation insurance. The positive news is that these programs exist; the negative news is that the income these programs provide will likely be insufficient to fully meet your financial needs. To supplement these programs and replace your full after-tax income, you should consider having private disability income protection of some sort. This insurance will usually pay, based on certain restrictions, about 65 percent of your pre-disability earnings or for limited policies a fixed amount until such time as you recover and can return to work or age sixty-five, whichever is the longer time period. You can get this insurance coverage by purchasing a personal policy from a life insurance company or, if your employer offers this type of coverage, buying a policy as part of an employee benefit plan through your company benefits election. My best advice to you is to seek a qualified life insurance agent to walk you through the best, most cost-effective strategy to obtain this coverage. It should be an essential part of your protection program to mitigate the risk of having a disability.

Many people do not purchase this type of insurance protection, as they believe they will not need it. In all likelihood, based on available statistics, they have a greater risk of becoming disabled at an early age than they do of dying prematurely. Disability events are real risks.

Another event that could occur that can take away the future income you have planned to use to pay your bills and save for your Fulfilling Stage is a major liability event. What I mean by this is: Suppose you are in a severe car accident and are the driver who caused the accident. Because of this accident, the person in the other car was injured and unable to work for an extended period. The injured driver will likely sue you for damages, and, in reality, many times these damages can exceed the coverage limits of your automobile insurance policy. What can you do to protect against this happening to you? Without sufficient insurance protection, the injured party is likely to sue you for damages and, if you do not have sufficient personal assets to pay the judgment, have the court mandate that payments come from your future earnings. To give you the enhanced protection you need, make sure your automobile policy has larger limits of coverage and purchase what is called a personal umbrella policy. These umbrella policies cost a few hundred dollars per year but give great peace of mind. You can find out how to purchase this coverage from your automobile insurance agent or company.

DEALING WITH DEBT

WHEN SHOULD PEOPLE USE DEBT?

In today's FinancialVerse, hopefully people use debt to get cash to buy carefully considered big-ticket, expensive things that they haven't saved to fully pay for or need to build their life such as a college education, a home, or a badly needed vehicle used to get to work. Or people may need temporary funds to help absorb the costs of an unexpectedly large medical issue or other unexpected cost that exceeds their emergency fund. The sellers of such big-ticket products and services know that what they are offering is very expensive, and they know that prospective buyers will need to finance the purchase. They have worked with prospective lenders to offer the financing needed. This type of borrowing makes sense to me, provided you can repay the loans with your cash inflow.

Contrast this type of borrowing with what we see today—where consumers use high-cost debt like credit cards, retail store cards, and payday loans to buy things they don't really need, pay current bills, or to maintain a lifestyle they cannot afford in the long term. This type of debt, when added to the debt taken on for big-ticket purchases, is sapping the financial strength of households. It is mortgaging their financial futures to pay minimum monthly payments and high interest rates for years and years.

Overall, when you add it all up, it is clear to me that we, as a society, are taking on too much debt of all types. In the FinancialVerse, you should only take on debt if you have carefully determined that the purchase is necessary and can easily repay the loan from your cash inflow. If you can't do that, you need to postpone or forego the purchase. That is common-sense reality.

UNDERSTANDING DEBT

Let's take a look at background information about the debt you will encounter in the FinancialVerse and what this debt can cost you. Before diving into how to deal with common kinds of debt, you need to familiarize yourself with the terminology used to categorize debt, so you know what you have:

➢ Secured Debts – These loans require use of collateral, like a house or car to back qualifying for the loan.

➢ Unsecured Debts – These loans require no collateral, like credit cards, retail store cards, or personal loans.

➢ Fixed Interest Rates – The loan has a fixed stated rate of interest (e.g., 4 percent) for the entire timeline of the loan, like a fixed-rate mortgage.

➢ Variable Interest Rates – The loan has a rate of interest tied to an index or reference such as the prime rate or interest rates set by the Federal Reserve Bank. This may cause the interest rate to change over the life of the loan, like credit cards or an adjustable rate mortgage.

➢ Fixed Loan Term or Repayment Period – These loans are set up to be paid off by a certain date, like a mortgage, student loan, or car loan. For example, the repayment term on a car loan could be forty-eight months.

➢ Variable Loan Term or Repayment Period – There is no set date by when the debt must be repaid, like credit cards and retail store cards. You can repay amounts in addition to the minimum required payment as you have the cash to do so.

➢ Deductible Interest – For these loans, interest paid may be tax deductible in certain circumstances. This would include loans like a mortgage or student loan. The government changes the type of loans and amount of interest that can be deducted. You should speak with your tax adviser to get the current update on deductibility of loan interest.

> ➤ Nondeductible Interest – For these loans, interest paid is not tax deductible. This would include loans like credit cards or a personal loan.

HOW MUCH DEBT SHOULD YOU HAVE?

Even if you can pay your debt with your cash inflow, having too much may simply eat up your free cash flow and cost a lot in interest and principal payments. This is one of the key financial risks you must avoid. Here are some things to consider when determining if you are taking on too much debt:

> ➤ Housing is the biggest monthly expense for most households. Limit your total housing costs, including mortgage or rent payments, real estate taxes, and homeowners or renters insurance, to a range. A good rule of thumb is to keep your housing costs around a third or 33 percent of your monthly income. It's just a rough gauge to make sure you have enough money for all the other necessities and to save for your Fulfilling Stage.

> ➤ Do not borrow money secured by your home unless you need it and can repay it from current cash flow. Remember: if you default on a mortgage, home equity loan, or home equity line of credit, there is a risk of losing your home.

> ➤ Student loan costs can be a significant outlay as well. As we have discussed, for both students and parents, it's important to consider how borrowing for college and beyond could

affect future plans. In my view, parents must consider funding their own Fulfilling Stage first, while students have to think about the reality of graduating with some debt.

MOST COMMON TYPES OF DEBT

Let's look at the four most common types of debt you will encounter in the FinancialVerse:

MORTGAGE DEBT

Houses are generally the most expensive purchase most people will make in their journeys. To make this big-ticket purchase, most people need to secure a mortgage on the property being purchased. There are a few different mortgage types to consider:

> ➢ FHA Loans – These are loans have been established to allow homebuyers with lower incomes to purchase homes. The Federal Housing Administration, or FHA, operates this loan guarantee program that allows homebuyers to buy a home with as little as 3 percent down. However, borrowers have to pay mortgage insurance costs to have the loan guaranteed by the FHA.

> ➢ Veterans Administration or VA Loans – Similarly, the Veterans Administration guarantees loans to service members and eligible surviving spouses. Loans backed by the VA might not require a down payment if the sales price is equal to or less than the appraised value. No private mortgage insurance

(PMI) is required, as the VA insures the loan. PMI is an insurance policy designed to protect the lender in case you can't pay your mortgage and default on the loan. Even if you have less-than-perfect credit, you may be able to get a loan at competitive interest rates.

➤ Conventional Loans – These loans are not federally guaranteed and are issued by financial institutions permitted to make such loans. Down payments of at least 20 percent of the purchase price are ideal, as down payments lower than this typically require private mortgage insurance, or PMI, which can be a significant, ongoing annual expense. Once your loan-to-value ratio hits 80 percent, PMI is no longer required.

➤ Home Equity Loans (HELOC) and Lines of Credit – These are loans designed to allow you to take out a loan based upon the equity you have built up in your home. The process of applying for a HELOC or home equity loan is similar to taking out a mortgage. An appraisal may be required, and the lender will evaluate your ability to repay. The home equity loan will be given to you in a lump sum, while the HELOC allows you to borrow against your home equity, up to the limit set by the lender.

Starting for the 2018 tax year, the interest paid on a home equity loan or HELOC will only be deductible if the related loan is used to buy, build, or improve the home securing the loan subject to certain limitations.

STUDENT LOANS

As we discussed in the section on student loans in the Adulting Stage, there are two types of lenders for student loans—federal and private.

> ➢ The federal government guarantees federal loans. They come with some benefits that may not be offered by private lenders, including income-driven repayment options, loan forgiveness programs, and fixed interest rates. Plus, some federal loans are subsidized, which means the government will foot the bill for the interest on the loan while the student is in school.

> ➢ Private loans come from banks, credit unions, or schools. In some cases, nonprofit agencies provide a guarantee for student loans, or lenders may self-insure. A private loan may have a variable interest rate, which means the interest rate you pay can change.

CAR LOANS

Many people need a car and make the decision to buy one. They quickly begin to understand that in comparison to owning a home or investing in an education, cars are a depreciating asset. As they repay the car loan, they are building little or no equity. Car loans can be obtained at banks, credit unions, and car dealerships. The average new car loan term can range from twenty-four to eighty-four months. The average loan term today is around sixty-five months per Autotrader (Autotrader.com).

For borrowers with great credit (FICO 8 scores between 781 and 850), the average new car loan rate was 3.17 percent at the end of 2017. On the other end, borrowers with the worst credit scores (between 300 and 500) got an average new car loan rate of 13.76 percent, according to Experian.

Besides the interest rate, be sure to check whether there are any penalties for early repayment. One thing to look for is whether the loan is calculated as simple interest, which lets you avoid paying interest if you're able to pay the loan off early. Alternatively, the interest could be precomputed, which adds the interest to your balance. If you pay the loan off early, you owe the interest you would have paid over the life of the loan. Or the lender may charge a fee called a prepayment penalty to let you out of the loan ahead of time.

My thoughts are that you should not buy more car than you need or can afford. If you shop based on securing a certain monthly payment, you may be setting yourself up for a problem down the road. Unless you're putting down a significant amount of money up-front, low monthly payments will typically come with long repayment plans—which add up to more interest paid over the life of the loan. Car loan terms have been stretching in recent years to accommodate higher car prices and consumer preferences. Long loan terms may also hinder your ability to sell the car before the loan is paid off if the amount owed is more than the resale value of the car. This is often referred to as negative equity or being upside down on your loan. Avoid buying a more expensive car than you can afford simply because you're able to finance it. Do shop around for a car loan before taking the loan offered by the dealership. Banks or local credit unions can many times offer you a better rate.

CREDIT CARDS

Credit cards can be great financial resources if used properly. They're convenient, easy to use, and may have valuable reward programs such as cash back percentages and rewards point/airline miles offers that can be exchanged for goods, services, and travel.

After you apply for a card, credit card issuers will review your credit report and decide whether they want to give you a line of credit. Depending on your income and credit history, lenders choose how much you are allowed to borrow and the rate of interest they will charge.

Most credit cards come with variable interest rates that are tied to the prime rate with rates of interest that can reach the mid-20 percent range. The prime rate moves up or down with interest rates set by the Federal Reserve.

Credit card issuers have many options for borrowers. Some cards offer balance transfers, some have great rewards, and some may be best for students or for those who are rebuilding their credit. Store-branded cards and gas cards may give you a break on purchases made at the store or gas station, but these cards sometimes carry higher-than-average annual percentage rates.

Overall, the best way to take advantage of credit cards is by not carrying a balance—that way, you get to reap all the rewards, but with none of the costs.

SUMMARY

Dealing with debt can be a very stressful and anxiety-producing experience. In the FinancialVerse, you should try to restrict your use of debt to big-ticket purchases and unexpected emergencies. Do not rely on debt to pay your monthly expenses and basic living needs.

For more information on how to deal with debt, please go to Debt.org. The website has great information on all aspects of obtaining, managing, and paying off your debt.

PROTECTING THE ASSETS YOU ACQUIRE OR USE

As you enter the Striving Stage and begin to generate a growing income, you will likely acquire possessions. Based on your individual choices, wants, and needs, you may purchase or rent a home, rent or buy a car, or acquire other assets such as video equipment, a video game library, or build a collection of vintage guitars. What happens if these possessions are damaged or destroyed because of fire, flood, or other circumstance? How do you get your money back to purchase a replacement?

There is insurance coverage for these risks, which is available from a property and casualty insurance agent or directly from selected companies. Based on the coverage you buy; you will receive cash from the insurance company to buy replacements. You can find out how to purchase this coverage from your property and casualty insurance agent or company. My advice is to work with an agent or company that will gather the information necessary to make sure you have coverage that is adequate for your financial circumstances.

CREATING AN EMERGENCY FUND

You can read the frequent headlines in the media stating that the vast majority of families can't come up with $400 to cover the cost of an unexpected bill. We also read that with average monthly expenses of about $5,000, most families have less than that amount in savings for an emergency. These are not things you want to do in the FinancialVerse.

My belief is that you should have at least six months of cash expenses on hand to protect you against the uncertainties of the FinancialVerse. The uncertainties include unexpected medical bills, the loss of your job, family emergencies, and home or car repairs. You can't rely on others for these needs; you have to prepare for them yourself. Overall, on a longer-term basis, I am an advocate of building an emergency fund over time that provides one year of expenses.

Building such an emergency fund does not happen overnight. You need to start out with small savings amounts and add to them as you can. My advice is everyone, even those at low-income levels, should work to have at least $10,000 on hand as a cushion against these uncertainties. I can tell you from personal experience that these events do happen, and you need to be prepared for them. Starting to build your emergency fund is one of the first things you need to do after you enter the Striving Stage. The first thing you should do is buy your parents or mentor a nice meal for all their support for you to get to the point where you can earn a reasonable living.

THE THREE-LEGGED STOOL OF SAVINGS
FOR THE FULFILLING STAGE

In the FinancialVerse, you need to accumulate savings and income benefits to generate the income you will need in the Fulfilling Stage of your financial life. Remember once you stop working, you will likely be in the Fulfilling Stage for twenty to thirty years. For younger adults, I believe thirty years should be your planning horizon.

These savings and benefits will likely come from three major sources—government programs, private savings, and from employer programs such as 401(k) plans and defined benefit pension plans. Many financial professionals refer to these programs as the three-legged stool of savings for later life. Let's briefly look at each leg of the stool.

GOVERNMENT PROGRAMS

Government programs include Social Security, Medicare, and Medicaid. These programs were designed to provide retirement, disability, and health cost benefits at certain ages or if certain events take place. A key understanding you must have is that these programs cannot be relied upon to provide the full amount of benefits you will need. For example, Social Security retirement payouts are designed to replace 40 percent of preretirement earnings for most people. **Not 100 percent, but 40 percent**. For higher-earning individuals, this percentage continues to drop as income earned increases. Medicare provides basic medical coverage but currently does not cover vision, dental, hearing, or long-term care benefits. Medicaid provides health coverage, but the insured has little if any say in where the care takes place. Remember, for the most part, the government dictates the specifics of coverage when it is responsible for paying the bill.

These programs are primarily funded and managed by the US government and the states. The current problem with these plans is that they look to be substantially underfunded by the government and will need to be modified in the near future. Social Security and Medicare have begun to run deficits—cash outflows are exceeding current contribution inflows. According to MACPAC (MACPAC.com), Medicaid programs run by the states made up approximately 28.7 percent of all state expenditures in 2015 and are showing an increasing trend. This large percentage is requiring cash-strapped state budgets to more carefully manage all payments for Medicaid patients.

These upcoming modifications to the government programs will likely include some cutback in benefits, lengthening of retirement ages, and some form of income means testing. These changes are needed to assure that all people get the necessary level of benefits from these plans.

I know that many younger adults believe these programs will not exist when they get to the ages to qualify for benefits. My belief is that these entitlement programs are too much of a political issue to be eliminated, but I do believe they will be significantly modified in the future, as noted above. I believe you can count on them in your planning for the Fulfilling Stage of the FinancialVerse but that you should build in consideration that their payouts to you will likely be less than you originally planned. This reduction in what these programs offer will place increased pressure on private savings and employer-provided benefits to fill in the gap.

PERSONAL SAVINGS – WHAT, WHEN, HOW MUCH?

Personal savings are the cash and investments you can accumulate in bank accounts, investments, 401(k) plans, IRAs, cash value life insurance, annuities, and income-generating assets from your earning activities, inheritances, or other sources. As you focus on savings, it is my belief that you will need to save as much as you can to supplement the future cash you will receive from government and employer programs. You will need to save as much as possible to fund your years in the Fulfilling Stage.

The key guideline that many financial experts discuss is to save at least 10 to 15 percent of your annual income. I believe that, given today's environment, you should save more if you can. The reason is that there may be years when you cannot put away 10 to 15 percent, and you need to plan for that contingency. You will need all the resources you can accumulate to pay for the costs of the Striving Stage, create an emergency fund, protect against your inability to earn an income, and prepare for the Fulfilling Stage of your journey.

You need to consider all the available product options and expense-savings techniques to maximize your personal savings. We will discuss these later in this book.

EMPLOYER PLANS

In the 1970s and 1980s, it was quite normal for the majority of companies to provide defined benefit or pension plans for their employees. These plans were designed to pay an annual cash income benefit of a percentage of the employee's salary after retirement for as long as the employee lived.

Individuals used to receive 50 to 60 percent of their preretirement earnings in pension income. These types of plans, however, are not available for the majority of today's workers.

Today, the number of companies providing these types of defined benefit plans has declined dramatically to the point where, according to Employee Retirement Benefit Institute, less than 25 percent of employers provide this type of benefit. Most employers have replaced these defined benefit plans with what are called defined contribution or DC plans. We will discuss these plans later in this chapter.

Participating in available employer plans is an essential element of accumulating funds for the Fulfilling Stage of your journey and must become a part of your planning. Taking full advantage of any funds that your employer will provide to you to assist in paying for your life after retirement is a must-do.

If you are self-employed, there are tax-qualified retirement programs in which you can participate and contribute to save for your later years. These plans vary, and you will need to consult a tax preparer, investment professional, life insurance professional, or other financial professional to assist you in establishing the plan that is best for you. As more and more people work as contractors or in the gig economy, these plans will gain favor.

SAVING AND INVESTING FOR THE FULFILLING STAGE

THE BIG FOUR TAX-ADVANTAGED STRUCTURES
CREATED TO HELP YOU SAVE

Before we discuss the major asset classes you can use to accumulate savings, it is important that you understand four tax-advantaged structures that the federal government has put in place to incent savings and paying for health care costs, funding education, and for the Fulfilling Stage of your life. The big four are:

➢ Health Savings Accounts (HSAs)

➢ 401(k) Plans

➢ Individual Retirement Accounts (IRAs)

➢ Section 529 College Savings Plans

These structures provide various tax incentives that can be obtained such as deductibility from current taxation for amounts contributed, tax deferral on earnings, or tax-free earnings. The federal government has created numerous such savings incentives, but we will not cover all of them. We will focus on the big four.

HEALTH SAVINGS ACCOUNTS (HSAS)

An HSA is a type of savings account that lets you set aside money on a pre-tax basis to pay for qualified medical expenses. By using untaxed dollars in a Health Savings Account (HSA) to pay for deductibles, copayments, coinsurance, and some other expenses, you can lower your overall health care costs.

An HSA can be used only if you have what is called a high-deductible health plan (HDHP)—which is generally any health plan (including an Obamacare/Insurance Marketplace plan) with a 2019 deductible of at least $1,350 for an individual or $2,700 for a family. The IRS sets and changes these deductible amounts each year. When you purchase health insurance plans, they are usually designated as "HSA-eligible."

Contribution and Out-of-Pocket Limits for Health Savings Accounts and High-Deductible Health Plans	
	2019
HSA contribution limit (employer + employee)	Self-only: $3,500 Family: $7,000
HSA catch-up contributions (age fifty-five or older)	$1,000
HDHP minimum deductibles	Self-only: $1,350 Family: $2,700
HDHP maximum out-of-pocket amounts (deductibles, co-payments and other amounts, but not premiums)	Self-only: $6,750 Family: $13,500
Source: IRS, Revenue Procedure 2018-30.	

HSA funds roll over year to year if you don't spend them. An HSA may earn interest, which is not taxable.

Some health insurance companies offer HSAs for their high-deductible plans. Check with your health insurance company for their offerings. You can also open an HSA through some banks and other financial institutions.

401(K) PLANS

A 401(k) is a federally designated retirement savings plan sponsored by an employer. It allows workers to save and invest a portion (usually up to a maximum of 15 percent) of their pay on a pre-tax basis. The money put into the plan is not company money but yours subject to certain restrictions. You do not need to worry that your employer can take your funds.

Federal and state income taxes aren't paid on the money deposited into the 401(k) plan until the money is withdrawn from the account. It is assumed you will be in a lower tax bracket once you start withdrawing the funds.

The key aspect with a 401(k) plan is that you direct and control how your money is invested. Most plans offer a wide range of investment options you can select for your money. These investments usually include money market funds, certificates of deposit, all types of mutual funds, and exchange-traded funds (ETFs).

To give you the benefit of not paying income taxes on the funds until withdrawal, the federal government, through the Internal Revenue Service (IRS), has put restrictions on what you can do with your 401(k). For instance, in most cases, you can't tap into your employer's contributions immediately. Vesting of employer contributions is the amount of time you must work for your company before gaining access to its payments to your 401(k). (Your payments, on the other hand, are always yours and vest immediately.) The fact that you can't immediately access your employer's contribution to your 401(k) is insurance against employees leaving early. On top of that, there are complex rules about when you can withdraw your money and costly penalties for pulling funds out before age fifty-nine and one-half.

To oversee your account, your employer usually hires an administrator like Fidelity Investments or Charles Schwab. They'll email you updates about your plan and its performance, manage the paperwork, and assist you with requests. If you want to keep watch over your account or shift your money around, go to your administrator's website or call their help center.

As part of making your savings hit the 10 to 15 percent target we discussed earlier, put as much as possible into the 401(k) plan to obtain the maximum employer matching contribution. Be mindful that you'll need to have enough money to live, eat, create your emergency fund, and pay down any excess debt you have. At the very least, you should contribute enough to get the full matching amount that your company pays. You don't want to leave free cash on the table. Nearly every plan offers matching funds—the most popular being 3 percent of your salary.

So how does a 3 percent employer match work? If you put in 3 percent of your $50,000 salary, or $1,500, your company puts in another $1,500 to match your contribution. For a company offering a 3 percent match, you can usually add more than that $1,500 yourself, but the company won't match beyond 3 percent. The rules for matching funds vary, so be sure to check with your employer about qualifying for its contributions.

The IRS sets maximum contribution limits for 401(k) accounts. These limits change each year. For 2019, the most you can put into your fund is $19,000 in any combination of pre- and after-tax dollars. If you're age fifty or older, you can add another $6,000 (this is to allow older individuals to make up for lost time and increase their retirement savings).

If your company offers a 401(k) plan, please read all the information before joining. Knowing the details of your company's plan will allow you to take maximum advantage of all the benefits the plan has to offer.

IRAS

An individual retirement account (IRA) is another structure that allows you to save money for retirement in a tax-advantaged way. It is different than a 401(k) plan. An IRA is an account set up at a financial institution that allows an individual to save for retirement with tax-free growth (a Roth IRA) or on a tax-deferred basis (a Traditional IRA). Like a 401(k) plan, there are restrictions on how the account must be set up, what types of investments are allowed, contribution limits, and how withdrawals can be accessed.

The three main types of IRAs each have different advantages:

- **TRADITIONAL IRA** – Contributions are made with <u>pre-tax</u> dollars you may be able to deduct on your tax return, and any earnings grow <u>tax-deferred</u> until you withdraw them in retirement. Many retirees find themselves in a lower tax bracket than they were in pre-retirement, so the tax deferral means the money may be taxed at a lower rate.

- **ROTH IRA** – Contributions are made with <u>after-tax</u> dollars, and any earnings grow <u>tax-free</u>, with tax-free withdrawals in retirement, if certain conditions are met.

- **ROLLOVER IRA** – The IRS allows you to use a Traditional IRA account for money "rolled over" from a qualified retirement plan. Rollovers involve moving eligible assets from an employer-sponsored plan, such as a 401(k) into an IRA, when the regulations allow you to do so.

The maximum IRA contribution limit for 2019 is $6,000 with those people over age fifty and older able to contribute an additional $1,000. Please note there are income restrictions on whether an individual can contribute to an IRA. Please consult your tax adviser for these contribution limits.

Whether you choose a Traditional or Roth IRA, the tax benefits allow your savings to grow, or compound, more quickly than in a taxable account.

WHY YOU SHOULD CONSIDER HAVING AN IRA

Many financial experts estimate that you may need up to 60 to 85 percent of your income to support your financial needs in the Fulfilling Stage. An employer-sponsored savings plan, such as a 401(k), might not be enough to accumulate the savings and generate the income you need. Fortunately, in many circumstances, you can contribute to both a 401(k) and an IRA, subject to the mandated income restrictions. An IRA can help you:

> ➤ Supplement your current savings in your employer-sponsored retirement plan.

> ➤ Gain access to a potentially wider range of investment choices than your employer-sponsored plan.

> ➤ Take advantage of potential tax-deferred or tax-free growth.

Try to contribute the maximum amount to your IRA each year to get the most out of this savings plans. Be sure to monitor your investments and make adjustments as needed, especially as retirement nears and your goals change.

529 COLLEGE SAVINGS PLANS

A 529 College Savings Plan (529 Plan) is an investment account that offers tax-free earnings growth and tax-free withdrawals when the funds are used to pay for qualified education expenses. The 529 Plan can also have financial aid benefits. 529 Plans may also be used to save and invest for up to $10,000 in annual kindergarten through grade twelve tuition payments in addition to college costs. There are two types of 529 Plans: college savings plans and prepaid tuition plans. Almost every state offers at least one 529 Plan. There is also a 529 Plan operated by a group of private colleges and universities.

529 PLAN TAX BENEFITS

Much like a Roth IRA, contributions to a 529 Plan are made with after-tax dollars and are not deductible for federal income taxes. However, the majority of participating states offer state income tax deductions or tax credits for contributions to 529 Plans, though you may be restricted to investing in your home state's 529 Plan in order to claim the benefit. Funds in a 529 Plan grow federal tax-free and will not be taxed when the money is withdrawn for qualified education expenses.

The funds in a 529 Plan are yours, and you can always withdraw them for any purpose. However, the earnings portion of a non-qualified distribution (not for qualifying educational expenses) will be subject to ordinary applicable federal and state income taxes and a 10 percent tax penalty, though there are exceptions. **Since your original contributions were made with after-tax money, they will never be taxed or penalized on these contributions.**

TYPES OF 529 PLANS

529 Plans are usually categorized as either prepaid tuition or college savings plans:

> ➤ College savings plans work much like a Roth 401(k) or Roth IRA by investing your after-tax contributions in mutual funds or similar investments. The 529 college savings plan offers several investment options from which to choose. The 529 Plan account will go up or down in value based on the performance of the selected investment options.

> ➤ Prepaid tuition plans let you prepay all or part of the costs of an in-state public college education. They may also be converted for use at private and out-of-state colleges. The

Private College 529 Plan is a separate prepaid plan for private colleges, sponsored by more than 250 private colleges. Educational institutions can offer a prepaid tuition plan but not a college savings plan.

WHAT EDUCATION-RELATED EXPENSES ARE COVERED?

At the college or post-secondary level, a general rule of thumb is that expenses required for enrollment in an eligible institution are covered. There are some costs, however, that you may believe are necessary, but the IRS does not consider a qualified expense. For example, a student's health insurance, transportation costs, and student loan payments are not considered qualified expenses.

Qualified expenses do include tuition and fees, books and materials, room and board (for students enrolled at least half time), computers and related equipment, Internet access, and special needs equipment for students attending a college, university, or other eligible post-secondary educational institutions. The 2017 Tax Cuts and Jobs Act also expanded the allowable use of 529 Plan assets by permitting tax-free distributions of up to $10,000 per year, per beneficiary, to pay for kindergarten through grade twelve tuition expenses at private, public, and religious schools.

CHANGING CIRCUMSTANCES

When it comes to putting money into a 529 Plan, many parents are concerned about what will happen in the future when their child is ready to attend college. In particular, some parents worry about losing the money they have saved in a 529 Plan if their child doesn't go to college or gets a scholarship. There is a myriad of situations that can arise in the future such as the death of a child, the receipt of full academic or athletic scholarships, or the receipt of employer educational assistance. These and many other situations require research and understanding of the regulations surrounding 529 Plans. A good online source I have found is SavingForCollege.com. This website covers the gamut with all issues relating to 529 Plans and is a great place to start your research.

Remember, you can withdraw leftover money in a 529 Plan for any reason. However, the earnings portion of a nonqualified withdrawal will be subject to taxes and a penalty, unless you qualify for one of the exceptions in the regulations. If you are contemplating a nonqualified distribution, be aware of the rules and options rules for reducing taxes owed. My advice is to consult your personal tax adviser before taking such a withdrawal.

THE MAJOR ASSET CLASSES

Overall, depending on which financial professional you speak with, there are between five and ninety different asset classes or subclasses in which you can put your money. In the FinancialVerse, you will commonly encounter the following asset classes:

> ➢ Real estate, including a personal residence

> ➢ Cash value life insurance products

> ➢ Government securities

➢ Savings accounts

➢ Corporate bonds and notes

➢ Common and preferred stocks

➢ Mutual funds

➢ Commodities

➢ Crypto-currencies

➢ Life insurance products

How much to put into each asset class and which classes to use to meet your individual goals need to be discussed in-depth with the financial planner you decide to use. I want to emphasize that in the early part of the Striving Stage, you should focus on building your emergency fund and putting the minimum insurance plans in place to protect your family and income.

Here are the major classes of savings and investment products you will encounter in the FinancialVerse:

➢ **REAL ESTATE** – Real estate is property made up of land and the buildings on it, as well as the natural resources that are part of the land, such as livestock, water, and mineral deposits. Although the financial media often refers to the "real estate market," from the perspective of residential properties, real estate can be grouped into three broad categories based on its use: residential, commercial, and industrial. Examples of residential real estate include undeveloped land, houses, condominiums, and townhouses; examples of commercial real estate are office buildings, warehouses, and retail store buildings; and examples of industrial real estate include factories, mines, and farms.

➤ **GOVERNMENT SECURITIES** – A government security is a bond issued by a government or governmental authority with a promise of repayment upon maturity. Government securities such as savings bonds, treasury bills, tax lien certificates, and notes also promise periodic interest payments. These investments are considered low risk, since they are backed by the taxing power of the governmental authority that has issued them. This could be a local, state, or federal government entity or authority. Almost all government securities are backed by the full faith and credit of the issuing jurisdiction.

➤ **SAVINGS ACCOUNTS** – A savings account is a place where you can store cash securely while you earn interest on your money. Unlike investment accounts, savings accounts are federally insured up to a limit, currently $250,000 per account. This federal insurance protects the money in your bank, credit union, or investment brokerage account if the financial institution holding the funds became insolvent. There are specific rules on how federal deposit insurance applies, and you should consult that information to fully understand the insurance. Using a savings account creates some distance between everyday spending money kept in your checking account and cash that's meant for a later date, like your emergency fund.

SAVINGS ACCOUNTS CAUTIONS

Here are some cautions relating to savings accounts:

➢ Savings accounts protect your money and can help it grow. The bank or other financial institution pays you interest on the amount you have on deposit. Savings accounts are lower-yielding, fixed-rate products.

➢ A major criticism of savings accounts is that they only pay small returns on the amount on deposit. For most of the past decade, interest earned on savings accounts has been less than 1 percent. This is starting to change, as interest rates have begun to rise again. To obtain a higher rate of interest on your account, look to online banks. These banks don't have to support expensive brick-and-mortar branches and large staffs of people, enabling them to offer more competitive annual percentage yields. These accounts also tend to have low initial deposit requirements and typically don't charge monthly maintenance fees.

➢ Savings accounts are designed to help you store money that you don't need immediately. This little restriction may help you leave the funds in place for their intended use.

HAVING AN EMERGENCY SAVINGS ACCOUNT FUND

It's smart to keep your emergency fund of six months' worth of living expenses in a savings account in case of job loss or other emergencies, which we discussed previously. Saving as little as $400 can get you out of many minor financial scrapes. Aim for $400 and build to the six-month level.

In my opinion, after you build an emergency fund of at least six months of living expenses and have that amount in your savings account, you can begin to invest for your Fulfilling Stage. You will be able to use the other asset classes we have discussed in this section to make those investments.

OTHER SAVINGS ACCOUNT PRODUCTS

Banks, credit unions, and brokerage firms offer other savings products to choose from, including:

➢ Money market accounts, which often require a higher minimum balance and in return offer a slightly better rate. These accounts might also come with a debit card or the ability to write checks.

➢ Certificate of deposit, or CD, which holds money for a fixed term, anywhere from a few months to a few years. The rate earned is usually higher the longer the amount is on deposit. Open a CD only with money you won't need immediately because withdrawing money before the end of the term usually carries a penalty (typically three to six months foregone interest).

FINDING THE BEST SAVINGS ACCOUNTS

If a basic savings account is what you need, start your search by looking at online banks and credit unions. These types of financial institutions keep fees to a minimum, offer high rates, and might even offer special tools to help you manage your savings. Once you've decided on a bank, you can open a savings account online or at a branch, where you'll need to provide a government-issued identification and other pieces of information, including your Social Security number, phone number, and address.

> **BONDS** – Bonds are obligations of companies that can be purchased for investment. There are numerous types, amounts, structures, and collateral backing bonds. Individuals purchase bonds as an investment to earn interest income.

> **STOCKS AND EQUITIES** – Stocks or equities represent fractional ownership in a company/corporation. For example, you might own ten shares of Apple Computer. People and businesses own stock because they want to share in the profits and value of the underlying business. Over time, it has been shown that returns to owners of stock can be the highest of any investment they can make. You can also lose most or all of your investment in stocks and equities if their value declines. These instruments have higher risk in exchange for higher potential return.

There are numerous types or classes of stock. The ownership rights that each type of stock has are determined by the company issuing the instrument and by the federal and state laws that govern the creation and issuance of the shares.

> **MUTUAL FUNDS** – A mutual fund is an investment consisting of different stocks or bonds. A mutual fund allows the owner to combine their money with others to make investments in companies. This often allows the mutual fund owner to use smaller amounts of investment dollars to make investments in many companies. This should reduce the risk to the owner of investing in individual companies. The mutual fund owner also gains the expertise of the mutual fund investment manager to oversee all investment decisions.

There are numerous types of mutual funds and mutual fund companies. All products and product sellers are subject to significant federal and state regulation and oversight over their sales, marketing, and other business practices.

Mutual fund products can be purchased from mutual fund companies and have specific rules as to when they can be purchased, sold, and when they are taxed for federal and state income tax purposes.

> **COMMODITIES** – Commodities are reasonably interchangeable goods or materials which are sold as an article of commerce. Commodities include farm products; fuels such as oil and natural gas; and precious metals such as gold, silver, platinum, and copper. Commodities are usually traded in bulk on a commodity exchange or on the spot market.

➤ **CRYPTO-CURRENCIES** – Crypto-currencies are any form of currency that only exists digitally and that usually has no central issuing or regulating authority such as the US Treasury or European Central Bank but instead uses a decentralized system to record transactions and manage the issuance of new units. These currencies rely on cryptography to prevent counterfeiting and fraudulent transactions.

Examples are Bitcoin, Ethereum, Litecoin, Ripple, and Dash.

➤ **LIFE INSURANCE PRODUCTS** – Life insurance products are contracts with an insurance company to pay you certain benefits if you die, become disabled, or request periodic payments. In their purest form, in exchange for cash payments, called premiums, the insurance company provides a lump-sum payment, known as a death benefit, to beneficiaries of the policy upon the insured's death or other event.

Typically, the type of life insurance product chosen is based on the needs and goals of the owner. For example, term life insurance generally provides protection for a set period (e.g., ten, fifteen, or twenty years), while permanent insurance, such as whole and universal life, provides lifetime coverage. It's important to note that death benefits from all types of life insurance are generally income tax-free.

For example, if you took out a life insurance policy on your life with a death benefit of $300,000, that is the amount the insurance company would pay to the people or entity that you have named as the beneficiary of the policy—income tax-free upon your death.

There are many varieties of life insurance products. Some of the more common types are discussed below:

TERM LIFE INSURANCE – Term life insurance is designed to provide financial protection for a specific period, such as ten or twenty years. With traditional term insurance, the premium payment amount stays the same for the coverage period you select. After that period, policies may offer continued coverage, usually at a substantially higher premium payment rate. Term life insurance is generally less expensive than permanent life insurance.

Term life insurance proceeds can be used to replace lost potential income during the earning years. This can provide a safety net for your beneficiaries and can also help ensure the family's financial goals will still be met—goals like paying off a mortgage, keeping a business running, and paying for college.

Term insurance does not, except in very rare cases, accumulate cash. It is designed to pay a lump sum benefit or a number of benefit payments in the future if the insured dies. It provides cash for future delivery. It needs to be looked at in such a way.

UNIVERSAL LIFE INSURANCE – Universal life insurance is a type of permanent life insurance designed to provide lifetime coverage. Unlike whole life insurance, universal life insurance policies are flexible and may allow you to raise or lower your premium payment or coverage amounts throughout your lifetime. Additionally, due to its lifetime coverage, universal life typically has higher premium payments than term.

Universal life insurance is most often used as part of a flexible protection, estate planning, and retirement strategy. Another common use is supplemental retirement income replacement. Some universal life insurance product designs focus on providing both death benefit coverage and building cash value, while others focus on providing guaranteed death benefit coverage.

In recent years, life insurance companies have added innovative new benefits to these policies that allow the cash accumulated in the policy to be used to generate tax advantaged retirement income or pay for long-term care expenses.

WHOLE LIFE INSURANCE – Whole life insurance is a type of permanent life insurance designed to provide lifetime coverage. Because of the lifetime coverage period, whole life usually has higher premium payments than term and universal life. Policy premium payments are typically fixed, and, unlike term, whole life builds cash value, which functions as a savings component and accumulates tax-deferred over time.

In recent years, life insurance companies have added innovative new benefits to these policies that allow the cash accumulated in the policy to be used to generate retirement income or pay for long-term care expenses.

Comparing Types of Life Insurance

	Term Life Insurance	Universal Life Insurance	Whole Life Insurance
Financial Need Covered	Cash for future delivery in the Striving Stage	Cash for future delivery, wealth transfer, income protection, supplemental retirement income, and some designs focus on tax-deferred wealth accumulation	Cash for future delivery, wealth transfer, preservation, supplemental retirement income, and tax-deferred wealth accumulation
Protection Period	Designed for a specific period (usually a number of years)	Flexible; generally, for a lifetime	For a lifetime
Cost Differences	Typically less expensive than permanent	Generally more expensive than term	Generally more expensive than term
Premium Type	Typically fixed	Flexible	Typically fixed
Proceeds Paid to Beneficiaries	Yes, generally income tax-free	Yes, generally income tax-free	Yes, generally income tax-free
Investment and Interest Rate Crediting Options	No	Can offer numerous funds depending upon the product type	Can offer numerous funds depending upon the product type
Builds Cash Value Accumulation and Long Term Care Protection	No	Yes, various riders available to help offset long-term care risk	Yes, various riders available to help offset long-term care risk

HOW ARE LIFE INSURANCE PREMIUMS CALCULATED?

Insurers use rate classes, or risk-related categories, and the amount of coverage requested to determine your premium payments. The underwriting process results in rating categories that do not affect the length or amount of coverage. Insurers gather evidence such as your and your family's medical history, credit history, lifestyle, and driving record as part of the application process. Your rate class is then determined. For example, taking certain prescribed medications or using tobacco could increase risk and, therefore, cause your premium payment to be higher than that of someone who doesn't have these situations.

ANNUITY PRODUCTS – An annuity contract is a written agreement between a life insurance company and a customer in which the insurance company promises to pay certain benefits as outlined in the agreement to the consumer in exchange for the premium paid. These benefits can be paid starting right away or can be received in the future.

The annuity contract outlines each party's obligations. Such a document will include the specific details of the contract, such as the structure of the annuity (variable or fixed investment returns), any surrender charge penalties for early withdrawal, beneficiary provisions, and other contract benefits or expenses.

There are federal and state income tax benefits to an annuity contract in that all income earned by the contract is tax deferred until such time as it is withdrawn from the contract. There are restrictions and tax penalties for accessing annuity benefits prior to age fifty-nine and one-half.

In recent years, life insurance companies have added innovative benefits to these products that create more ways for income to be earned within the contract and optional benefits that can be purchased to allow for more control over how and when income is received. Lastly, newer contracts offer some innovative ways to pay for long-term care expenses using the cash accumulated in the annuity contract.

An annuity contract is beneficial to the individual in that it legally binds the insurance company to provide a guaranteed periodic payment to the person designated as the annuitant when that person reaches a certain age and requests commencement of payments. Essentially, it guarantees income for life.

ANNUITY PURCHASE CAUTIONS

Annuities can be complex, and annuity contracts may not be suitable for some buyers due to their individual circumstances. Here are a few cautions to keep in mind when shopping for an annuity:

- Be sure to understand that annuity contracts usually have surrender charges for early withdrawal of your money in the contract. Be sure to understand the amount, duration, and when the charges apply.

- Understand how income is earned on the contract and credited to you. Sometimes insurers offer high teaser rates to encourage buyers followed by far lower rates for the life of the annuity contract. The way around this is by having the annuity seller be clear on the rate they will pay for the life of the annuity.

- Annuity contracts are medium- to long-term products. You should not purchase a contract with cash you could need in the short term. While annuity contracts offer limited liquidity provisions, they are not designed to be liquid like a checking account.

- Understand the liquidity provisions of the annuity contract, including how much can be withdrawn each year without penalty and what, if any, provisions allow withdrawal of funds in case they are needed for a long-term care event or to pay for costs if you are diagnosed with a terminal illness.

- Lastly, the issuing life insurance company backs up the guarantees included in the annuity contract. Know the company you are doing business with and their financial strength ratings.

THE RISK/RETURN TRADE-OFF SPECTRUM

As you better understand the various asset categories, you will find that each comes with what is called a risk/return trade-off. The chart below presents a graphical representation of each class and the potential for cash return and the related risk to generating that return. For example, if you put your money into US government bonds, the likelihood of the government defaulting on the bond is next to zero. The return on this asset class is lower, however. Compare that to putting your money into an equity stock mutual fund where the annual return potential is much higher, but the principal is at risk to market value swings. If you are a conservative person, putting the money into government bonds might better fit your needs. That is the trade-off—a lower return in exchange for the guarantee of your principal. Your financial professional will work with you to assess your risk appetite and work to recommend to you the investment classes that best meet your needs.

The following chart illustrates the risk return spectrum for several different product types including cash, government securities, fixed deferred annuities, fixed index annuities (FIA) with and without guaranteed lifetime withdrawal benefits, variable annuities (VA) with and without guaranteed lifetime withdrawal benefits, bond funds, mutual funds, and stocks.

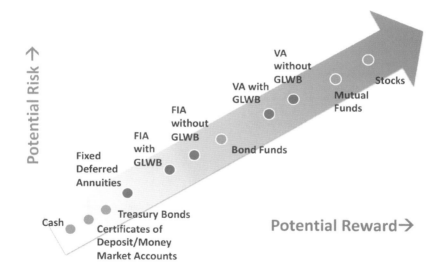

Potential Risk – Potential Return Spectrum

STAGE SUMMARY

The Striving Stage of the FinancialVerse is the time when you will earn the income that will support your financial life. You will make most of the key decisions and take related actions that determine the quality of your financial life and prepare you for the Fulfilling Stage. Keys to this stage include:

➤ Knowing where you stand financially by religiously using a budget

➤ Understanding all the new and innovative ways the assets and services you need can be acquired

➤ Making disciplined decisions on how you use debt to create the quality of life you desire

➤ Creating an emergency fund

➤ Consistently saving to accumulate assets and income streams that will fund the Fulfilling Stage of your life

➤ Understanding the major asset classes you can purchase with your savings

➤ Maximizing your use of tax advantage savings programs that are available to assist you in accumulating assets for later in life and paying for key necessary expenses

➤ Protecting your income, assets, and potentially creating a legacy using insurance products

CHAPTER 5

THE FULFILLING STAGE (OVER AGE SEVENTY)

What happens after you have worked for thirty to forty years and followed the ideas presented in this book? You will likely have successfully navigated your financial journey and have accumulated savings and income streams for your later life. What happens next? You are now entering the Fulfilling Stage of your financial life.

Today, most Americans look to enter this stage of their financial lives in their late fifties or early sixties. Unfortunately, many people are coming to the sad realization that they cannot afford their desired lifestyle and activities based on what they have saved and invested. It is my belief that based on today's lengthening life expectancies, personal debt loads, and the increasing daily cost of living for older ages (particularly the cost of health care), most people are looking to enter this phase of their lives in their late sixties or early seventies. That is why I believe the Fulfilling Stage of financial life begins after age seventy for most people.

The Fulfilling Stage usually begins when your full-time employment earning years are over and you embark on what many say is your retirement. I don't like the concept of retirement, as it does not properly describe what happens in people's lives. It is a dated concept.

In my opinion, today, most adults will likely enjoy this stage for twenty to thirty years—from age seventy to age ninety or later. I believe most Baby Boomers should plan on living until at least age ninety. Younger adults should plan to break the one-hundred-year-old mark based on continued medical breakthroughs. More and more, I believe there will be no such thing as a formal age when we stop all meaningful work or charitable activity. I believe people will simply move from full-time work to a period of part-time work, charitable activities, and more time for personal pursuits. They will remain active until a much higher age, and will have more control over their time.

PLANNING CONSIDERATIONS

As you plan for the Fulfilling Stage of your journey, think through your personal values, along with key economic, psychological, and emotional considerations. Try to define these as early as possible in your planning.

These considerations will impact your planning and guide how much you will need to save to fund your needs in this stage. The major considerations of the Fulfilling Stage usually are:

> ➢ How long do you want or are able to continue to work for money? Will you switch to part time in your current job, start a business, or look to be a contractor/consultant?

> ➤ What do you want to do with your post-earning years? How active do you want to be? What charitable efforts will you support? Will you get more involved in your community?

> ➤ What is the state of your health? What are your ongoing medical costs? Are you taking many prescription drugs?

> ➤ How long do you project you will live? Does your family have a history of long-life spans? Shorter life spans?

> ➤ What do you want to leave, if anything, as a financial legacy for your family, church, college/university, or favorite charity?

> ➤ What lifestyle do you plan on having and maintaining as you cease full-time work? Will you go out to dinner five nights per week, or will you eat at home each night? Will you travel extensively or stay closer to home?

> ➤ What are your family responsibilities? Are you raising or financially supporting your grandchildren? Are you a caretaker for aging parents or an ill child/family member?

> ➤ What are your debt service demands? Do you still have a mortgage? Are you paying your own or your children's student loans?

The questions are many but need to be carefully thought through to properly plan for the Fulfilling Stage of your financial life.

LIVING COST CONSIDERATIONS

As you plan your journey through the Fulfilling Stage, paying for the costs of living become more and more important. You must fund these costs from the income and assets derived from the combination of your personal savings, employer-provided retirement plans, and governmental programs from the three-legged stool we discussed earlier.

To properly plan, you need to have a good understanding of your housing, transportation, food, health care, entertainment, charitable support, travel, and other financial commitments such as support for adult children or grandchildren. Many financial planning professionals say that in the Fulfilling Stage, you will need less money because your living expenses in your later years decline. As someone who is in their later years, I can tell you some categories of expenses do decline while others increase, and some new types of costs emerge (e.g., Medicare supplement and long-term care insurance premiums). The best approach I think you can take is to look at your planned expenditures in two major buckets—discretionary and nondiscretionary—and plan accordingly. This approach will help you deal with the reality of no longer working full time and the other activities you are planning.

Let's look at how these costs—discretionary and nondiscretionary—break down.

DISCRETIONARY COSTS

I have heard Tom Hegna, the nationally recognized speaker on retirement income (TomHegna.com), discuss the key phases of later life that need to be planned for. These phases are the go-go, slow-go, and no-go phases. The exact timing of these phases differs for each person based upon his or her personal needs, health, and family circumstances. These phases directly affect your discretionary expenditures and how much you need to save to fund them.

For example, you see many people postpone traveling until they reach older ages, during which they book several cruises per year, travel on group trips, or visit places in the world they have always wanted to see. These are the go-go people. On the other hand, there are people who cannot visit the places they want or do the things they had planned because of health or caretaking responsibilities—the no-go crowd. Another consideration is the person who has led an active life and traveled extensively and wants only to give back or donate their time and money to charitable causes they feel strongly about. Each person needs to plan a different amount of discretionary spending in retirement. One pattern is clear, and that is as a person ages, the discretionary expenditures usually lessen.

If your plans are to make charitable contributions of your time or money as part of your Fulfilling Stage, you need to plan for these years ahead to have the necessary funds set aside.

NONDISCRETIONARY COSTS

According to the latest Bureau of Labor Statistics data for the year 2016, "older households"—defined as those run by someone sixty-five and older—spend an average of $45,756 a year, or $3,813 a month. That's $1,059 less than the monthly average spent by all US households combined, as we demonstrated in the Striving Stage.

A widely accepted rule of thumb that financial professionals use in planning is that you'll need to replace between 60 and 85 percent of your income to maintain your standard of living in the Fulfilling Stage. But your actual spending will depend on a number of factors, including what you decide to spend on nondiscretionary items and the lifestyle you choose.

Here's the BLS data shown as a monthly breakdown of how households headed by a person age sixty-five and older spend money, on average, in seven major categories:

• Housing: $1,322
Certain housing costs never go away, even when you have paid off your mortgage. This monthly expenditure includes property taxes, insurance, utilities, repairs, maintenance, and household supplies.

• Transportation: $567
The $6,814 annual average outlay, which includes the costs of gas, insurance, maintenance, and repairs, is about one-third less than the nearly $9,252 average households of other ages spend each year.

- Health care: $499

These costs are about 27 percent greater than what younger households incur. This should be expected as medical costs typically increase as we age. It also shows the impact of having to pay Medicare-related insurance premiums and more health-related costs.

- Food: $483

Older individuals spend nearly 20 percent less than the average household does on food.

- Personal insurance/pensions: $237

These costs are calculated to drop over 40 percent when compared to younger households.

- Cash contributions: $202

Older families report dedicating $2,429 of their annual income to "cash contributions" (which include charitable donations), compared with $2,088 by the average household.

- Entertainment: $197

Here, older households continue to spend on entertainment as they settle into their Fulfilling Stage, but somewhat less than the broader average ($243 a month).

A key reminder when looking at these projected costs is that the BLS estimates include the normal activities of daily life but do not include paying for large discretionary items, major charitable gifts of time and money, and major out-of-pocket items such as health care costs. Health care costs are the financial wild card of preparing for the Fulfilling Stage.

THE HUGE POTENTIAL IMPACT OF HEALTH CARE COSTS

The cost category that has the best chance of causing unplanned and increasing annual spending in the Fulfilling Stage is health care. You can look forward to spending between $6,000 to $15,000 per year in health-care-related costs for Medicare-related insurance premiums, doctor bills, prescription costs, private insurance premiums, dental costs, and vision costs. The higher annual amount is much higher that the BLS shows, but I think the higher number may better reflect the reality of medical costs today.

This amount is supported in an October 2018 Research Issue Brief from the Employee Benefit Research Institute (EBRI). The brief shows that a couple sixty-five years old with median prescription drug expenses would need $296,000 in cash savings to have a 50 percent chance of having enough on hand to cover their health care costs. If the couple wanted to have 90 percent certainty of covering the costs, they would need to have $400,000 in savings. This EBRI cost estimate does not include long-term care costs, other expenses not covered by Medicare, and the possible impact of modifications to what Medicare covers that will likely come from Congress. These costs are the Fulfilling Stage's wild card expense as far as I am concerned. If you are lucky and have great health in your later years, you may need less money. If you fall into poor health, your costs could skyrocket. In my view, unless Congress makes a bipartisan effort to reform Medicare, costs will continue to increase well above the overall rate of inflation.

PLANNING FOR THE COSTS OF LONG-TERM CARE

Genworth Insurance, one of the nation's leading private long-term care insurers, predicts that two-thirds or 66 percent of people over age sixty-five will incur long-term-care-related costs in their lifetimes. Long-term care costs can be significant.

For the last fifteen years, Genworth has developed the Cost of Care Survey to help families understand the costs of varying types of care across the US. Since 2004, the Cost of Care survey has become the foundation for long-term care planning for many individuals. The 2018 survey, conducted by Carescout, covering 440 geographical regions, is based on data collected from more than 15,500 completed surveys.

Here are the estimated annual median costs for a number of long-term care related expenses taken from the 2018 Genworth Cost of Care Study:

ANNUAL NATIONAL MEDIAN COSTS 2018

Homemaker Services (based on forty-four hours per week): **$48,048**

Home Health Aide (based on forty-four hours per week): **$50,336**

Adult Day Health Care (based on five days per week): **$18,720**

Assisted Living Facility (based on twelve months of care, private, one bedroom): **$48,000**

Semi-Private Room in a Nursing Home (based on 365 days of care): **$89,297**

Private Room in a Nursing Home (based on 365 days of care): **$100,375**
Genworth 2018 Cost of Care Survey, conducted by CareScout®, June 2018

As you can see, the costs of long-term care services can be substantial. With an ever-aging population and with more and more people needing cognitive or memory care, the reality of this cost is sobering. The most startling disclosure, however, is given these substantial costs, most people believe the costs are fully covered by the Medicare program, **which they are not.**

Once individuals determine there are little if any Medicare benefits, they are confronted with the reality of having to pay for these long-term care costs. They then seek out state-regulated Medicaid coverage for their needs. When they do, they then get the second unwelcome surprise. To qualify for Medicaid coverage, they will have to exhaust or spent down almost all of their savings, excluding home equity, to qualify for coverage. Each state has its own requirements for the spend down of assets and what assets can be retained by the person entering the long-term care facility paid for by Medicaid. The surprises don't end there. Lastly, if the person does financially qualify for Medicaid, the state determines the standard of care and approves which long-term care facility where the patient is admitted. The patient loses control of their care in exchange for state involvement.

The major lesson here is that you need to set aside cash for the costs of long-term care in retirement or purchase some form of private long-term care insurance coverage. This is becoming more and more evident to aging Americans.

Long-term care insurance coverage comes in various amounts with significant restrictions on coverage. In the last few years, the life insurance industry has developed many new long-term care products along with new long-term care alternative products that have a wide variety of coverage and cost options. You need to see a qualified life insurance agent with a specialty in long-term care insurance to get the right coverage.

Overall, you need to get some form of protection against the risk of a long-term care event. If not, you are placing your family and others in the position of having to care for you, if needed.

GENERATING INCOME

As you plan for the Fulfilling Stage, your financial focus will change from accumulating assets and income benefits to generating income from these sources. I believe unless you have received a financial windfall at an early age, this planning should not take place any later than age fifty. My advice is to meet with a financial professional to review and assess all of your income options and related decisions.

This planning effort should address a number of key considerations including:

> ➢ The best time to collect income benefits from Social Security

> ➢ Considering application for a reverse mortgage

> ➢ Timing to file for benefits of employer plans

- ➤ Understanding the income to be generated from personal assets

- ➤ Understanding the process of applying for Medicare benefits and health coverage

- ➤ Debt management

- ➤ Identification of legal issues relating to the process.

Getting advice on generating income is a must in my view. Professionals have the background and experience to help you maximize the amount and tax advantaged nature of income in your later years.

STAGE SUMMARY

The Fulfilling Stage of the FinancialVerse should be just that – the stage of your financial life where you receive both the psychological and financial benefits of a life well-lived and planned. Keys to this stage include:

> ➤ Properly planning for the activities and charitable actions you desire to take in later life

> ➤ Understanding how to properly protect against rising healthcare costs

> ➤ Preparing to properly fund the costs of living, including providing for long-term care, medical, and nondiscretionary items

> ➤ Working with a financial professional to establish the income streams needed to fund what will likely be an increasing life expectancy.

CHAPTER 6

USING THE POWER OF GUARANTEES TO SUCCEED

WHAT ARE GUARANTEES?

Guarantees are legal agreements that one party promises the other that they will perform—a service, a financial transaction, or a certain action such as the replacement of a defective product—even if they lose money on that performance. Manufacturers, banks, insurance companies, delivery services, and other entities offer them. The good news is they are available, and they can provide you with significant benefits. The bad news is they have a cost that can be significant. In my view, there are certain guarantees available in the FinancialVerse where the benefits significantly outweigh the cost.

You will see in the financial media a barrage of articles questioning the cost of having guarantees in place or if the company/person offering the guarantee will actually live up to their promise to perform. I am here to tell you that guarantees are for the most part very good if you select the right products and companies. You want to have them in your toolbox for your journey.

As an example, I think one risk you can work to minimize using guarantees is the risk of living too long and running out of cash. The ramifications of running out of money to live on in old age are horrible given your likely inability to go to back to work to support yourself. You don't want to wear a chicken costume outside a restaurant, do you? Is there a guarantee you can purchase to protect you against this risk? How can you plan to minimize this risk? What is the cost of this guarantee?

To protect yourself against the risk of outliving your money or what is called longevity risk, you have several options:

1. Rely on family members or friends to get you the cash or caretaking help you need.

2. Rely on government programs such as Social Security.

3. Purchase a private insurance product from a state-regulated life insurance company called an annuity that will guarantee that a certain amount will be paid to you for as long as you live.

4. Pay the costs out of your private savings.

For most people, private savings are not enough, as they do not have sufficient assets to assume the risk of having to pay for the costs themselves. Totally relying on Social Security is not enough, as Social Security is designed to replace about 40 percent of preretirement income, as we noted previously. Getting cash from family and friends is possible, but the question arises: can you rely on them for as long as you live? Lastly, buying a lifetime income guarantee using an annuity can be a great solution to minimize the risk.

In its simplest form, to purchase this product, which is called an income annuity, you pay a lump-sum premium to the life insurance company in exchange for the insurance company's promise to pay you a certain amount each month or year for the rest of your life or a period of time that you choose (e.g., twenty years). How can the life insurance company make good on this promise? How are they able to do this for you when you can't do it for yourself? The key is that the insurance company has buying power to purchase higher-yielding assets than you can; they can provide this service for large numbers of people, some of whom will die in younger years, providing funds for those who live longer, and they have the technology and actuarial talent to manage the risk that you do not.

There are costs to providing guarantees. They are not free. They are in some instances subsidized by the US government for the good of the economy. What they do provide to you are ways to minimize or eliminate risks from your financial journey. For some reason, you will not see much written in the financial media about the power of guarantees. Yet, the psychological solace you get with the knowledge money or a replacement product or service will be delivered in the future, if it is needed, is powerful and comforting.

TYPES OF GUARANTEES

There are many types of financial, product, and service guarantees available. Examples include:

> **DEPOSIT INSURANCE** – This is insurance provided by the federal government that will pay you up to a certain limit if the financial institution where you have placed your money becomes insolvent. Coverage is $250,000 of insurance for each account you have with the institution. For more information, see FDICInsurance.com.

> **LIFE INSURANCE** – This is a guarantee that the insurer will pay the person or entity you have designated a certain amount upon your death. For example, if you have a $250,000 policy, it will pay that amount upon your death. That is the guarantee. Life insurance companies are regulated by the states to maintain their solvency and ability to pay claims promptly.

> **INTEREST RATES** – Banks, insurance companies, and other licensed deposit-taking financial institutions can guarantee to pay you a certain rate of interest, say 3 percent, on deposits you have with them in checking accounts, savings accounts, annuities, and life insurance products.

> **PRODUCT AND SERVICE GUARANTEES** – These are guarantees that if a product or service is deficient or does not work as promised, you can get your money back or a replacement product. The

entity backing the guarantee is usually the company providing the product or service.

> **CREDIT LINES** – Banks, savings and loans, or credit unions usually issue credit lines. The issuing company guarantees that you can obtain funds up to your established limit for certain costs as agreed. For example, a bank may extend to you a line of credit backed by the equity in your home to use however you desire.

> **OVERDRAFT PROTECTION** – Overdraft protection is offered by banking institutions. It allows you to take more out of your checking account than you have on deposit up to certain limits. This guarantee can come with a cost.

> **FIRE INSURANCE** – Fire insurance is a guarantee to pay certain amounts to you if your home, rental property, or other structure is destroyed by fire. You pay an amount, called a premium, and the insurer agrees to pay you a certain amount if the fire takes place.

Guarantees are numerous. They come with a cost. Some are costlier than they should be. They each offer a benefit for you. Look into them, understand what they can provide you to reduce financial risks, and buy those that meet your financial and psychological needs.

CHAPTER 7

FINDING FINANCIAL ADVICE

As we have discussed, the key decisions you need to make and the problems you will face in the FinancialVerse can be complex, confusing, and rapidly changing. In my view, to have a successful journey, you should get competent advice along the way. The good news is despite public reports to the contrary, there are high-quality, cost-effective, federally and state-licensed financial professionals available to help you. The bad news is due to our financial regulatory system, your ability to get all the advice and services you need for your journey from one source or person is almost impossible.

The reason for this is that the individuals or firms may not have all the regulatory permits and licenses to provide the services and products you need. You will usually need to go to at least four sources—a financial planning professional, a life insurance agent (for life, health, and disability insurance coverage), a general insurance professional (for home, property, and liability coverage), and an investment professional (for securities investments). We are also seeing the rise of Internet-based financial advice services for individuals who want to make self-directed decisions using the technology support these services provide. My advice is to seek out trusted people you can talk to, to start your journey. After you have the basic guidance you need, you can make the decision to begin to make direct decisions on your planning, protection, and investment needs.

FINDING ADVICE

To find these professionals, please go to the websites of the certifying organizations and professional associations such as the Certified Financial Planner Board of Standards (CFP Board), the Society for Financial Services Professionals, the Financial Planning Association, the American Society of Certified Public Accountants, or the National Association of Insurance and Financial Advisors to learn more about financial advisers in your area.

In the FinancialVerse today, you will encounter roughly two hundred financial adviser designations, according to Financial Industry Regulatory Authority (FINRA), one of the financial industry's self-regulating organizations. FINRA has research material that will allow you to decode most of the letter designations of financial advisers through accessing the FINRA website at FINRA.com. The alphabet soup of credentials can seem confusing when you're seeking advice. Please be certain you understand the credentials and experience of the person you are dealing with.

WHAT IS A FIDUCIARY?

Experts in consumer protection in the personal-finance field advise consumers to work with advisers with designations that require financial professionals to be fiduciaries.

"A fiduciary relationship requires advisers to act in the best interest of the clients and to avoid conflicts of interest, or fully disclose and manage all conflicts or potential conflicts," Pamela Banks, senior attorney at Consumer Reports, is quoted as saying in a November 15, 2018, press release titled "What Do the Letters After a Financial Adviser's Name Really Mean?" This release was made by Consumer Reports and is available at ConsumerReports.org.

While certain financial professionals are required by law or the rules of their professional affiliation to be fiduciaries, most, such as stockbrokers, life insurance agents, and general insurance agents, are not. Those professionals who are not fiduciaries conduct their business in accordance with the federal and state regulatory laws and mandates. These govern what products they are approved to sell, what services they can provide, what consumer disclosures are required, and that the products offered must have a reasonable basis for them making a purchase recommendation to you. They are required to be state and, in some cases, federally licensed. These licensing requirements mean they have met the educational, specialized knowledge, experience, and continuing education standards for the license(s) they hold.

Beginning in 2019, you should expect to see new state and federal regulations mandating a fiduciary or fiduciary-like approach for more and more types of financial services.

Some professional licenses have more requirements than others. For example, a candidate looking to become a chartered financial consultant (ChFC), for instance, pledges to "make every conscientious effort to ascertain and understand, render that service which, in the same circumstances,

I would apply to myself," according to the chartering organization, the American College for Financial Planning.

But even when a professional takes that vow, there may be times when he or she is permitted to stray from it. For instance, an adviser who is a certified financial planner (CFP) must act as a fiduciary when providing specific services like retirement or estate planning, but not necessarily when picking investments. That conflict between the two roles occurs particularly when a stockbroker also is a CFP. To address this, the CFP Board of Standards has revised its ethical code and standard of conduct to require a CFP to follow a fiduciary standard for all financial advice, as of October 2019.

The bottom line is to work with professionals who will act in your best interest and choose someone whose specific training and expertise aligns with your needs. Look for reviews of their service online and be inquisitive about how they treat their clients.

WHAT KIND OF ADVICE DO YOU NEED?

Below is a list of financial services you may seek in the FinancialVerse and the types of advisers best suited to help. The information provided below changes, so please go to the websites of the noted organizations for the most up-to-date information.

> **GENERAL FINANCIAL PLANNING** – Certified financial planners (CFPs) can give guidance on investing, saving for retirement, drawing down savings during the Fulfilling Stage, buying

long-term care insurance, financing college, estate planning, getting the right type of mortgage, and other personal-finance issues. CFPs must have a bachelor's degree—or higher—from an accredited college or university and three years of full-time personal financial planning experience or the equivalent in part-time experience (two thousand hours is considered one full-time year). They must take a certifying exam. They must take thirty hours of continuing education every two years. They must adhere to a code of ethics and standards of conduct.

➢ **COMPLEX LIFE INSURANCE AND ESTATE PLANNING** – Chartered financial consultants (ChFC) work similarly to CFPs, but holders typically have more training in insurance and estate planning, in a quote attributed to Don Blandin, president and CEO of Investor Protection Trust, a nonprofit devoted to investor education. Candidates need to have three years of full-time business experience within the five years before they receive the designation. They need to pass a number of courses taught by the governing body—The American College of Financial Services. They take a certifying exam. They must take thirty hours of continuing education every two years.

➢ **INCOME TAX EXPERTISE** – These are certified public accountants who also have taken coursework and passed a separate examination on financial planning to carry the title CPA/PFS, for personal finance specialist. They can offer income tax and personal financial-planning services as well.

Before sitting for an exam for personal financial planning, CPA/PFS candidates must take seventy-five hours of related courses within the five-year period. They must have the equivalent of three thousand hours of full-time business or teaching experience in personal financial planning. As CPAs, they're required to pass the state examination and to take continuing education courses, specified by the state in which they're certified.

➤ **BUDGETING AND DAILY FINANCE** – An accredited financial counselor (AFC) can address a variety of financial challenges, including debt reduction and family finances. These counselors do not sell investment products but rather help their clients learn the process of saving and investing and help them develop strategies for reaching their long-term financial goals.

Candidates must have one thousand hours of financial counseling experience, submit three letters of reference attesting to their professional competence and experience, and take self-study courses and an accrediting exam (undergraduate course work or professional experience may also be acceptable in lieu of the self-study courses). They must take thirty hours of continuing education every two years.

➤ **LIFE, HEALTH, DISABILITY, AND LONG-TERM CARE INSURANCE** – You should consult a life insurance agent. Life insurance agents are individuals who are licensed by a state or states to sell life, disability, health, long-term care, and certain other types of coverage. Many other types of advisers (e.g., stockbrokers or certified financial planners) may also be licensed to sell or provide advice on these insurance products. There are different types of insurance agents with some only able to offer the products of their company (exclusive agents), while independent insurance agents sell products of two or more insurance companies.

Life insurance agents have to pass state licensing examinations specific to the products they offer, continue to take continuing education courses, pass product training requirements from the insurance carriers they represent, and, in most cases, have errors and omissions insurance coverage in place. Agents offering Medicare-related coverages are subject to additional sales, product, and market conduct requirements.

> ### HOMEOWNERS, RENTERS, VEHICLE, AND PERSONAL UMBRELLA INSURANCE
– You should consult a general insurance agency or property and casualty insurance company. General insurance agents are individuals who are licensed by a state or states to sell all property and casualty insurance coverages. Many other types of advisers (e.g., life insurance agents, stockbrokers, or certified financial planners) may be licensed to sell or provide advice on general insurance products. There are different types of insurance agents, with some only able to offer the products of their company (exclusive agents), while independent insurance agents sell products of two or more general insurance companies.

General insurance agents have to pass state licensing examinations specific to the products they offer, continue to take continuing education courses, pass product training from the insurance carriers they represent, and, in most cases, have errors and omissions insurance coverage in place.

➤ **PURCHASE OF STOCKS, BONDS, MUTUAL FUNDS, AND EXCHANGE TRADED FUNDS (ETFS)** — Dealing with individuals who hold the chartered financial analyst (CFA) designation in addition to their mandated state and federal securities licenses is a good idea. To take the CFA certification exam, candidates must enroll in a CFA education program, hold a bachelor's (or equivalent) degree or be in the final year of a bachelor's degree program, or have four years of professional work experience, among other requirements. The CFA Institute's code of ethics and standards of professional conduct says, "Members and candidates must act for the benefit of their clients and place their clients' interests before their employer's or their own interests."

Other individuals or entities you will see in the investment field include:

ROBO-ADVISERS — Robo-advisers are a new class of financial adviser that can provide financial planning, investment advice, or investment management online using technological resources to support the service or advice provided. These services provide digital financial advice based on mathematical rules or algorithms. These algorithms are executed by software, and, thus, financial advice does not require a human adviser. The software utilizes its algorithms to automatically allocate, manage, and optimize clients' assets.

There are a growing number of robo-advisory services that are targeted to people who want to make their own investment decisions. Investment management robo-advice is considered a breakthrough in formerly exclusive wealth management services, bringing services to a broader audience with lower costs compared to traditional human advice. Robo-advisers typically allocate a client's assets on the basis of risk preferences and desired target return. While robo-advisers have the capability of allocating client assets in many investment products such as stocks, bonds, futures, commodities, and real estate, the funds are often directed toward ETF portfolios. Clients can choose between offerings with passive asset allocation techniques or active asset management styles.

REGISTERED INVESTMENT ADVISERS – Registered investment advisers (RIAs) are fiduciaries which specialize in investments; they typically deal with clients with $500,000 or more in investable assets.

RIAs are individuals or firms that provide advice for a fee on various types of investments as their full-time job. These individuals are registered and licensed by the US Securities and Exchange Commission (SEC) or appropriate state securities or financial regulatory agencies. An investment adviser must have the proper license to sell or give advice on securities products.

STOCKBROKERS – Stockbrokers, frequently called registered representatives, are licensed by the federal government and the state(s) in which they practice to purchase and sell securities products such as stocks, bonds, ETFs, and mutual funds. They typically receive commissions for the sales of these products. They are subject to oversight and compliance requirements that are dictated by federal, state, and industry self-regulatory entities.

INVESTMENT MANAGEMENT COMPANIES – There are a number of investment management companies such as Fidelity, Charles Schwab, and Vanguard, which create, manage, or sell investment products such as mutual funds, ETFs, stocks, bonds, and insurance products on a direct basis to the consumer. These companies offer a significant number of resources using their web-based technology. These resources include transaction execution, financial calculators, investment-related information, demographic data, and research materials.

HOW DO YOU PAY FOR ADVICE?

There are four main ways that financial professionals are compensated for the advice they provide. They are:

> ➤ Through hourly rates paid directly by you for the time taken or project requested.

> ➤ Commissions paid directly by the investment or insurance product provider to the financial professional.

> ➤ Fees paid directly by you (e.g., 1 percent on all investments managed by the adviser).

> ➢ Through subscription services. These are just being introduced into the market and will require the payment of flat monthly fees in addition to a reduced level of directly paid fees. You should expect much innovation in this area in the years ahead.

Hourly rates are self-explanatory and are usually charged by the financial professional based on a rate schedule they provide. The total charge for the service will be based on the complexity of the plan or project and related time spent.

If your adviser receives payment from the investment or insurance product provider that he or she sells you, they are usually receiving an up-front commission. Rather than your adviser receiving compensation directly from you, the investment, life insurance, or general insurance company they're recommending for you pays them for the sale and marketing costs of their product. Just because they receive a commission does not mean you overpay for the service received. Most advisors will disclose the commission they receive to you as part of the sales process. Commissions on insurance protection products can range from 15 to 100 percent of the first-year premium. Commissions on investment products and cash value life insurance products such as annuities usually range from 1 to 7 percent of the amount invested.

Commissions can create potential conflicts of interest that can be harmful to the investor. The fiduciary standard we discussed above mandates that an adviser is legally bound to providing the highest standard of care and must always put his or her client's interests above their own. It aims to prevent advisors from making product recommendations and investment decisions solely based on the up-front payments or commissions they will receive.

HOW ARE FIDUCIARY ADVISERS PAID?

Fiduciary advisers are paid directly by you their client, but the fees that are paid can come in different forms. Clients might pay a financial-planning fee as discussed above. This financial plan could cover topics such as cash flow planning, Fulfilling Stage income planning, debt reduction, college planning, insurance planning, and more.

You are hiring the adviser on a project basis to take a few hours of their time to understand your goals and create a plan to show you how to accomplish those goals. You might also agree to pay a monthly fee to work with this adviser on an ongoing basis to help you stay on track with your plan.

The most common fee-based compensation method advisors are using today is charging a fee based on the investments they manage for you. Say, for example, this fee is 1 percent. If you have a $250,000 portfolio and you pay your adviser 1 percent, then you are paying them $2,500 per year, or $250,000 multiplied by 1 percent. Fees of this type typically range from 0.6 to 1.5 percent, although they vary.

UNDERSTANDING COMMISSIONS AND FEES

The difference between paying commissions versus fees is in the incentives they create. An adviser who receives commissions is inherently incentivized to recommend products that pay the highest commissions. An adviser who charges a financial planning fee or an investment-management fee is incentivized to grow the assets you have given them to manage. This is because they only continue to receive their fee if your assets grow in value and if you stick around and keep working with them. Keep in mind that in many cases, paying an up-front commission may be better economically than incurring ongoing annual costs depending on the product purchased, the amount of annual service needed, and your time horizon.

How can you find out what that fee is? Ask and read the disclosures provided to you.

A 1.25 percent advisory fee might not sound like a lot. But what does that represent on a $250,000 account? It comes out to $3,125 per year. It could be that your adviser is providing that much value to you and your plan. However, these costs must be clearly disclosed to you when you start working together. If you don't know what you're paying your adviser and you are curious, ask them directly. They should provide you with a fee schedule.

Most advisers today operate as what is called a "fee-based" adviser. Not to be confused with a "fee-only" fiduciary adviser, a fee-based adviser can charge clients under either the commission structure or fee structure. Depending on the client and situation, a fee-based adviser can choose whichever payment structure he or she would like. Don't assume that because your adviser says they're fee based; it means they legally must put your best interests ahead of their own.

Always understand what you are paying in commissions or fees and the how the amounts are calculated and paid.

ADMINISTRATIVE COSTS AND EXPENSES

Just because you know how your adviser gets paid doesn't mean you know the full amount of costs you will incur for your investments. Usually there are additional amounts paid for other costs and expenses involved in investing your money. These costs exist whether you work with an adviser or not, but you should understand how to keep these costs as low as possible.

Anytime you buy or sell a stock, mutual fund, or ETF, you might be paying a trading cost. These costs can range from five dollars per trade up to fifty dollars per trade. The trading costs on your funds will depend on where you hold your investments (e.g., TD Ameritrade, Fidelity Investments, Charles Schwab, etc.). These companies, known as custodians, make their money through trading costs, so it's important that you work with a custodian that keeps costs low.

Another cost is the internal expense of managing the mutual funds. Pay attention to this one. Unless you enjoy reading through pages and pages of regulatory prospectus materials (the legal language that outlines the fees, objectives, and performance history of mutual funds and ETFs), then you probably don't know the actual internal cost of the funds you're invested in.

What is an internal cost? It's the cost associated with the management and operation of the mutual funds or ETFs you invest in. All mutual funds and ETFs have an internal expense. You need to understand what these are and make sure your adviser is aware of how they will impact the performance of your investment.

WHY DO YOU NEED A COACH?

As I indicated above, unfortunately, due to how our government has chosen to regulate the purchase of financial services, you will likely need to go to several companies and related entities to buy the products and services you need. Here are some examples:

> ➢ To purchase or establish banking services such as checking accounts, savings accounts, personal loans, mortgages, or car loans, you will need to go to a bank, savings and loan, credit union, or finance company that is licensed to sell these products.

> ➢ To purchase a financial plan, go to a financial planner, preferably a CFP. At the same time, other professionals such as insurance agents, registered investment advisors, banks, accountants, or stockbrokers can offer such a service and software tools to create a plan for you. The CFP is usually best equipped to deliver this service in a comprehensive manner based on their training, continuing education, and professional standards.

> ➢ To purchase general insurance products, go to a property and casualty insurance agency or agent. This entity and its representatives can sell you automobile insurance, homeowner's coverage, and personal liability products.

➢ To purchase life insurance, disability, health insurance, and annuity products, go to a life insurance agency or agent. This entity and its representatives can sell you these products.

My view, based on my personal experience, is that as you start your journey into the Striving Stage of the FinancialVerse, you need to create a team of a financial planner, a life insurance agent, and a general insurance agent to guide your journey. This team should be able to provide you with the advice you need to put the foundation plans and protections in place. As you proceed through the Striving Stage and your needs become more complex, you will need to add other resources to your team including a CFP, an attorney, and other professionals.

CHAPTER 8

LIFELONG FINANCIAL LEARNING

THE NEED FOR LIFELONG FINANCIAL LEARNING

I can't stress enough that you need to spend at least two hours per week viewing, reading, or listening to financial-related news and information. To become an educated traveler in the FinancialVerse, you must understand the economic environment we face, the news events impacting your money, the products and services available, and the consumer trends moving the markets. I get my information from a variety of sources. I am a regular viewer/listener of CNBC, Bloomberg, and Fox Business Channel. In addition, below are my suggestions for reference sources for you to read or listen in addition to what you have learned from the FinancialVerse.

Here are my recommendations.

WEBSITES THAT CAN HELP

I have selected sites that I believe focus more on personal financial issues versus those that look at starting a business, entrepreneurial ideas, and business management. There is a tremendous amount of free information available from these sites that can make your financial journey better each day. Find one or two you really like, and consistently visit them.

- ➤ Kiplinger.com

- ➤ Money.com

- ➤ MarketWatch.com

- ➤ CNBC.com

- ➤ Yahoo Finance

- ➤ NerdWallet.com

- ➤ Bankrate.com

- ➤ WiseBread.com

- ➤ MyMoney.gov

- ➤ BankingSense.com

- ➤ CashMoneyLife.com

- ➤ ModestMoney.com

- ➤ HumbleDollar.com

- ➤ SeekingAlpha.com

PUBLICATIONS WORTH THE READ

I read four financial publications on a regular basis, reading the daily, weekly, or monthly issues of the publication. They provide great sources of information, practical ideas, and suggested strategies for what can be done with money and how to address certain financial risks.

The publications are:

- ➤ The Wall Street Journal

- ➤ Kiplinger's Personal Finance

- ➤ Forbes Magazine

- ➤ Money Magazine

PODCASTS OF IMPORTANCE

I am an avid listener to podcasts and subscribe to about thirty on a regular basis. What are podcasts? For those of you who haven't joined the trend yet, think of them as seven- to thirty-minute audio or radio programs you can listen to when you want and as often as you want. You can listen to them on your phone, desktop, or tablet while you drive, exercise, or walk.

I usually listen to them as I complete my morning walk. If you are new to podcasts, you can subscribe to them using Apple Podcast, Google Play, iTunes, Spotify, SoundCloud, and the Stitcher applications, for example. These applications are free to access and use.

I have chosen these podcasts based on my experience with the quality of topics discussed and keeping my interest. My recommendations are:

- ➤ This Morning with Gordon Deal

- ➤ Planet Money Series

- ➤ *The Economist Series*

- ➤ The Dave Ramsey radio program and podcasts

- ➤ *Optimal Finance Daily*

- ➤ *Radical Personal Finance*

- ➤ *Money for the Rest of Us*

- ➤ *Listen Money Matters*

RESOURCES YOU SHOULD CONSIDER IN YOUR EDUCATION

There are a number of other financial resources available on an online basis to assist you with your journey including financial-planning software, financial calculators, detailed product information, retirement income, and investment-planning applications.

These applications can be obtained from your local banking institution, LifeHappens for life-insurance-related materials, Life Insurance Marketing and Research Association (LIMRA), the Employee Benefit Research Institute (EBRI), the Bureau of Labor Statistics (BLS), and from investment management companies such as Fidelity and Charles Schwab.

SUMMARY

I cannot stress enough that you should spend my recommended two hours per week on your financial education. In my opinion, the key reason people fail in their financial journeys is that they didn't have the necessary education and information to make the key financial decisions in their lives. People go through life financially illiterate and expect things to get better for them when in fact they have not taken the actions to educate themselves. Today so much quality information, advice, and ideas are available on the Internet, podcasts, blogs, and the general financial media that can really help people make the decisions they need to make in the FinancialVerse.

CHAPTER 9

ACTIONS TO TAKE
AFTER READING THIS BOOK

I am a firm believer that you change your financial life by changing your financial mindset. After reading this book, you should be able to clearly see and understand what your financial journey should look like. Now it is time to take action to improve your journey.

Where are you in your journey? Have you protected yourself against the eight financial risks? Do you have an emergency fund? It is time to stop, assess where you are, and map out your steps going forward. Here is the nine-step program I suggest:

1. Decide what you want your journey through the FinancialVerse to look like.

2. Begin your two-hour-per-week education program.

3. Make a financial asset inventory.

4. Make an inventory of your outstanding debts and obligations.

5. Prepare a budget for the next year or update your existing budget.

6. Get a general insurance checkup.

7. Get a life, health, and disability insurance checkup.

8. Get a Fulfilling Stage checkup to see where you are in accumulating assets, electing benefits, and generating income for this stage of your life.

9. Identify and meet with your initial coaches depending on your needs.

Let's discuss how you should approach each action.

ACTION 1 –
DECIDE ON YOUR GOALS FOR THE FINANCIALVERSE

This is the first step in your journey and the hardest for most people. If you are married or in a relationship where you are jointly responsible for financial matters, this would include sitting down with your partner and having a careful and thoughtful conversation.

The purpose of this conversation should be to agree on your collective approach to money. Where are you today? What do you want your financial journey to look like? What lifestyle do you want to have? Where do you want to live? What college do you want to attend? Do you want to be a multimillionaire? Do you want maximum free time? Do you want to live in a major city? Do you like rural areas? Do you want to travel extensively? Do you want to be a fashion leader or a fast follower of key trends? Do you have special needs that must be considered such as caring for an aging or ill parent or family relation?

If you are older and in the midst of your Striving Stage, take a hard look at where you are, your prior relationship with money, and determine what actions you need to take to get on the track you want.

I think the best way to go about this action is to write down your four or five key goals and try as best you can to understand the costs of each lifestyle decision. Unfortunately, almost every one of your lifestyle and purchase decisions comes with a financial implication.

DETERMINING THE FINANCIAL COST OF YOUR DESIRED LIFESTYLE

An analysis created by USA TODAY and published on July 4, 2014, provides an example of what you need to consider in setting your goals. The article shows that living the American dream (i.e., owning a home, taking an annual vacation, owning an SUV) would cost the average family of four about $130,000 a year. Only sixteen million US households—around one in eight—earned that much in 2013, according to the US Census Bureau.

With that in mind, USA TODAY added up the estimated costs of living the American dream as follows:

> ➢ Home ownership is central to the American dream. So, they took the median price of a new home ($275,000), subtracted a 10 percent down payment, then projected the annual cost of a thirty-year mortgage at 4 percent interest. They also added annual maintenance costs of 1 percent of the purchase price. Total: $17,062 a year.

> ➢ They used the US Department of Agriculture's April 2014 figure of $12,659 for a moderate-cost grocery plan for a family of four.

> ➢ They used the May 2014 cost estimated by the American Automobile Association or AAA of $11,039 a year to own one four-wheel-drive sport-utility vehicle.

> ➢ Medical costs were calculated using the Milliman Medical Index of annual health insurance premiums and out-of-pocket medical expenses at $9,144.

> ➢ They used various estimates for the costs of restaurants and entertainment, one family summer vacation, clothing, utilities, cable or satellite, Internet and cell phone, and miscellaneous expenses.

> ➢ Total federal, state, and local taxes were pegged at 30 percent for households at this income level, based on a model developed for Citizens for Tax Justice.

➢ USA TODAY calculated current educational expenses for two children at $4,000 a year and college savings (all of it pretax) at $2,500 per year per child, based on various rules of thumb.

➢ Finally, USA TODAY estimated the maximum annual pretax contribution to a retirement plan for people under fifty to be $17,500. That's slightly less than 15 percent of this American dream household's annual earnings.

All of this adds up to a total of $130,357 in annual expenditures.

It sounds like a lot, and you might disagree with the methodology they used in a country where the median household income is about $51,000, but I think it is a great representation of what I am trying to communicate about the FinancialVerse. Everything comes with a financial cost. Add one more child and another vehicle to the above analysis, and you could easily reach the family needing to earn $150,000 after-tax annually to finance their definition of the American dream. The key is to reasonably know what your lifestyle costs.

There can be big regional variations, too. It costs a lot less to live the American dream in, say, New Mexico or Alabama than it does in metro areas like New York and San Francisco, where housing prices and taxes are sky high.

ACTION 2 –
BEGIN YOUR TWO-HOUR-PER-WEEK
EDUCATION PROGRAM

My recommendation is that you can start this action by visiting one of the sources for podcasts and subscribe to four podcasts, as mentioned in Chapter 8. I would also access applications for CNBC, Fox Business, *The Wall Street Journal*, and Dave Ramsey to read each week. These sources, along with being a faithful listener to the podcasts for the *Economist, This Morning with Gordon Deal*, and *Optimal Finance Daily*, will provide you with more information than you need to begin your financial journey. This sampling of content will also allow you to decide which programs deliver the most value for the time spent listening.

ACTION 3 –
MAKE A FINANCIAL ASSET INVENTORY

Make a detailed listing or inventory of all your financial assets as of a certain date including cash in the bank, savings accounts, retirement accounts, real estate owned, and other assets. Try to include the value of each of these assets as of the same date. This should give you a starting point of what you own and have accumulated so far in your journey.

ACTION 4 –
MAKE AN INVENTORY OF YOUR OUTSTANDING
DEBTS AND OBLIGATIONS

Make a detailed listing or inventory of all your outstanding debts, including credit cards, student loans, mortgages, retail store cards, car loans, and other outstanding obligations. Understand the terms and cost of each debt, as it will come in handy as you begin conversations with your coaches. Most people don't fully understand how much debt they have accumulated and what it is costing them in interest and principal payments.

ACTION 5 –
PREPARE A BUDGET FOR THE NEXT YEAR OR
UPDATE YOUR EXISTING BUDGET

Prepare a budget that lists all sources of your cash inflows and all cash outflows you are required to make. If you are one of the 28 percent of people who already have a budget, update what you have prepared for what you have learned about the FinancialVerse. My advice is to prepare a budget for the next twelve months.

If you would like help with how to prepare a budget and what to include, select one of the budgeting applications I listed earlier. As you meet with your financial coach, they may have a model or application they prefer for you to use.

ACTION 6 –
GET A GENERAL INSURANCE CHECKUP

Make a detailed listing or inventory of all your general insurance policies. This would include car insurance, homeowner's insurance, renter's insurance, personal liability insurance, accident insurance, and any personal liability umbrella coverage you may have in place. This information will be needed when you meet with your general insurance coach to assure you have the necessary coverage in place.

ACTION 7 –
GET A LIFE, HEALTH, AND DISABILITY
INSURANCE CHECKUP

Using the life insurance checkup form included as Appendix 1, take an inventory of all your existing life, health, and disability coverage in place. These will include those you get at work plus those you have purchased privately. Complete all required information for each policy, as it will come in handy as you begin your conversations with your coaches.

ACTION 8 –
GET A FULFILLING STAGE INCOME CHECKUP

Using the Fulfilling Stage income checkup form included as Appendix 2, take a complete inventory of all assets, pension plans, 401(k), or other benefits you have that will generate income for you to fund the needs of the

Fulfilling Stage. Complete all required information for each item listed, as it will come in handy as you begin your conversations with your coaches.

ACTION 9 –
SELECT AND MEET WITH YOUR FINANCIAL COACHES

Depending on your individual needs, you will need to interview and select your initial coaches. For most people, this will include a financial planning professional, a life insurance professional, and a general insurance professional.

After you have arranged meetings with each prospective coach, you can make a decision on which professionals best fit with your personality, needs, and budget. During your meetings with each person, your coaches will take the information you have accumulated and help you find solutions to your needs after considering the key financial goals you want to achieve. If you agree to work with the coach, you should also agree to meet with them at least annually thereafter to check the progress of your plan, products chosen, and how your needs have changed.

SUMMARY

Completing the nine-step action plan should provide you with an assessment of where you are with your financial journey, what actions you need to take to improve the quality of your journey, and peace of mind that you have protected yourself and your family to the maximum extent possible.

CHAPTER 10

FINAL THOUGHTS — YOUR LIFE IN THE FINANCIALVERSE

Today, most people are living extremely close to the edge of financial insecurity. Their cash income is just about equal to their cash living expenses, with most families reporting that they have little or no emergency funds to fall back on. Financial literacy and understanding of financial essentials are at low levels.

At the same time, we are just entering the Fourth Industrial Revolution and about to feel the forces of rapid and pervasive technological innovation with related impacts on our work and personal lives. The need to quickly acquire new work skills and pursue lifelong learning will be essential to continue to be employed and earn reasonable incomes.

The above considerations will make your financial life, in what I have called the FinancialVerse, to be more complex, confusing, and potentially stressful than ever before. If you don't have a basic knowledge of how the FinancialVerse works and don't spend time understanding money matters, you will likely live an anxiety-filled day-to-day existence. Even minor financial decisions will become painful to make. Major unexpected life events such as an illness or job loss will become financially and emotionally overwhelming.

To effectively deal with this environment and reduce the financial stress and anxiety in your life requires you to have a money mindset change. You need to take actions to embark on a path of lifelong learning, basic financial planning, and annual assessments of where you stand financially.

Throughout this book, I have tried to provide you with a framework to use to look at your expected financial life and make it simpler and easy to understand. I believe the best way to take a complex situation like this and make it understandable is to begin planning with what specific results you want to create. As presented in this book, you need to look at your financial life as you would any other problem you encounter in life.

Overall, to take charge of your FinancialVerse and reduce financial stress and anxiety, you should take a series of actions aimed at:

> Determining how you want to live financially.

> Understanding the major stages of your financial life—Adulting, Striving and Fulfilling—and what you can expect during each stage.

> Putting in place a financial budget that reflects your values, goals, and aspirations considering the stage you are in.

> Identifying and understanding the key financial risks you face.

➢ Putting protections in place to reduce or eliminate these financial risks.

➢ Investing a small amount of your time (only two hours per week) in lifelong financial learning using the abundant sources available from the Internet and financial media.

➢ Having the discipline to periodically assess your progress—at least annually.

➢ Securing good coaches to give you advice and help your decision making until you are able to make decisions on your own.

In *The FinancialVerse*, I have tried to:

➢ Identify what problems and risks you can expect to encounter.

➢ Walked you through how to think about each situation.

➢ Provided you with ideas on where to go to get advice and assistance when you need it.

I thank you for taking the time and making the investment in your personal financial literacy. My best to you as you seek to continue to improve your knowledge of money and how to manage it to provide the life you want. Remember: When in doubt, ask for help. There are a great number of qualified and professionally trained financial professionals and organizations who are there ready to help.

ABOUT THE AUTHOR

Harry N. Stout is a retired financial services executive with over thirty years of practical experience in all aspects of personal finance, banking, insurance, investments, and financial management. A certified public accountant by training, he has worked in countries worldwide helping consumers save, financially protect their families, and prepare for the later years of their lives. He has been the president and/or chief executive officer of several large US and international businesses. He has written for numerous financial publications, hosted national podcasts, and been seen on national television. He is acknowledged as a thought leader on personal financial management, retirement planning, investments, and life insurance.

Stout is a graduate of Drexel University in Philadelphia, Pennsylvania. He and his wife, Jennifer, reside on Daniel Island, South Carolina.

APPENDICES

APPENDIX 1 –
LIFE INSURANCE CHECKUP

Just as you have routine health, dental, and even car checkups, your life insurance could use an annual checkup, too. By taking time to review your current policies, personal circumstances, and changing needs, you may be able to:

- Save money on your life insurance premiums.

- Reduce your income tax liabilities with certain types of life insurance.

- Ensure that your life insurance and estate plan are in sync with changing tax laws.

- Add to or reduce the amount of life insurance you have.

- Make sure your policy is performing up to your expectations.

- Earmark policy proceeds for your favorite charities.

- Before you meet with your adviser, it will be helpful if you tell them about yourself and your family, the changes you've encountered over the past twelve months, and what you hope to accomplish during your checkup. Answer only the questions that apply to you. Not all of them will. Your responses will assist in finding potential solutions for your personal circumstances and interests.

CHECKUP FORM

PART 1: BASIC INFORMATION

Name _____

DOB _____

Client B Name _____

DOB _____

Child Name _____

DOB _____

Child Name _____

DOB _____

Address _____

Client A Contact Information

Daytime Phone _____

Evening Phone _____

Cell Phone _____

Email Address _____

Occupation _____

Business Name _____

Client B Contact Information

Daytime Phone _____

Evening Phone _____

Cell Phone _____

Email Address _____

Occupation _____

Business Name _____

Top Three Concerns

List your top three concerns you'd like to discuss during your life insurance checkup.

1. _____

2. _____

3. _____

PART 2: CHANGE CHECKLIST

Check all that apply to you and/or your family in the past year.

- ❏ Moved/changed address
- ❏ Have given birth to or have adopted a child
- ❏ Taken on any new dependents
- ❏ Became a grandparent
- ❏ Got married for the first time
- ❏ Remarried

- ❏ Separated from your spouse
- ❏ Divorced
- ❏ Had a change in health
- ❏ Have a family member with a change in health
- ❏ Stopped smoking or stopped using nicotine/tobacco

Residency Changes

- ❏ Moved to a new home
- ❏ Sold a home or apartment
- ❏ Taken out a home equity loan
- ❏ Refinanced your home
- ❏ Mortgage Amount _____

Professional Changes

- ❏ Changed employers
- ❏ Gotten promoted
- ❏ Started or purchased a business
- ❏ Closed or sold a business
- ❏ Changed a business partner

Insurance-Coverage Changes

- ❏ Made loans or assignments of your life insurance
- ❏ Changed beneficiaries on an of your life insurance policies
- ❏ Have become uncomfortable with the amount of life insurance you have
- ❏ Have had concerns about whether it is best for you to have term or permanent life insurance

Changed Life Insurance Companies:

Company _____

Policy Number _____

Insured(s) _____

Beneficiary(-ies) _____

Amount _____

Changed Health insurance Companies:

Company _____

Policy Number _____

Insured(s) _____

PART 3 FINAL QUESTIONS

Your answers to these questions can help the adviser address your needs and interests during the review process.

1. What was your annual income this past calendar year? _____
2. What is your anticipated income this upcoming calendar year? _____
3. What was your spouse's annual income this past calendar year?_____
4. What is your spouse's anticipated income this calendar year?_____
5. In the past year, have you changed or created a will or trust? _____

Future
Considerations
Check all that apply

❑ Additional life insurance for your or your spouse/ domestic partner
❑ Insurance for your children or grandchildren
❑ A special needs trust for a child or grandchild
❑ 529 plans for your children or grandchildren
❑ Gifts to charity
❑ Disability income insurance
❑ Annuities
❑ Long-term care insurance for yourself or spouse
❑ Long-term care insurance for your parents

Conclusion

Use the space below to comment on anything you'd like me to know before our meeting:

APPENDIX 2 –
FULFILLING STAGE INCOME CHECKUP

As you develop a strategy for your Fulfilling Stage and begin living in it, it is important to routinely estimate your expenses and determine how much income you'll need to live comfortably. It's never too early or too late to start! This simple guide may help you identify your needs and develop the information necessary to create a strategy for your future. It also provides you with a checklist you can use—whether you are years, months, or days away from your retirement date.

FULFILLING STAGE INCOME WORKSHEET

Start with this three-part worksheet to find out how financially ready you are for the Fulfilling Stage and to identify areas to help you be better prepared.

PART 1: Identify Your Essential Expenses and Lifestyle Expenses
Use this chart to pinpoint your current monthly expenses

Essential Expenses	Amount	Lifestyle Expenses	Amount
Housing	$	Dining out	$
Utilities	$	Clothing	$
Health care	$	Hobbies	$
Transportation	$	Entertainment	$
Groceries	$	Personal care	$
Insurance (life and other)	$	Charitable giving	$
Debts	$	Gifts	$
Income taxes	$	Professional services	$
Other	$	Other	$

Total Current Monthly Expenses: $_____

PART 2: Determine Your Fulfilling Stage Income

Use this worksheet to inventory the amount of monthly income you expect to receive from all sources.

Source	Amount	Source	Amount
Pension	$	Roth IRA	$
Social security	$	Brokerage account	$
Fixed annuities	$	Other savings	$
Variable annuities	$	Life insurance cash value	$
Veteran's benefits	$	Home equity	$
Long-term bonds	$	Employment income	$
Rental income	$	Interest and dividends	$
Employee savings plans	$	Municipal bonds	$
Traditional IRA	$	Other	$

Total Monthly Fulfilling Stage Income: $_____

Part 3: Calculate Your Income Replacement Ratio

You've estimated your current monthly expenses and sources of Fulfilling Stage income. How do you think these current expenses will compare to your needs in retirement? Do you expect the amount of these expenses be the same, lower, or higher during your later years? How much ordinary income will you need to replace with Fulfilling Stage income?

Consider this when you evaluate your replacement ratio. Most experts agree you'll need anywhere between 60 to 85 percent of your pre-retirement earnings to maintain your desired standard of living. So, your personal replacement ratio will depend on how you want to live during Fulfilling Stage. Consider the following examples based on $100,000 of annual Striving Stage income, which is $8,333 monthly income:

- If you want to live more modestly than you did before you stopped work, your replacement ratio will be lower than 100 percent.

- Example: 70 percent replacement ratio = $5,833 monthly income ($70,000 annually)

- If you want to maintain your current lifestyle, your replacement ratio will be 100 percent.

- Example: 100 percent replacement ratio = $8,333 monthly income ($100,000 annually)

- If you want to live larger than your current lifestyle, your replacement ratio will be more than 100 percent.

- Example: 120 percent replacement ratio = $10,000 monthly income ($120,000 annually)

Total Monthly Expense: _____ / Total Current Monthly Income:

_____ = Estimated Replacement Ratio:_____%

How long until you begin your Fulfilling Stage? Use this checklist to develop a strategy for your retirement as you work toward the big day.

A Few Years Before You Retire . . ...

- ❑ Define your Fulfilling Stage goals
- ❑ Maximize contributions to retirement accounts
- ❑ Take advantage of catchup contributions
- ❑ Ensure at least a portion of your income is protected
- ❑ Plan ahead for potential long-term care expenses
- ❑ Pay down debts

As You Get Closer to the Fulfillment Stage . . ...

- ❏ Review your benefits including healthcare benefits (if available)
- ❏ Evaluate and document your workplace retirement plan(s)
- ❏ Gather information about your Social Security benefits
- ❏ Investigate your Medicare coverage and Medicare Supplement options
- ❏ Pinpoint gaps in your health care, income, and other important benefits
- ❏ Reassess and estimate your income needs
- ❏ Create a Plan B for the unexpected (illness, unplanned work event, income gaps)
- ❏ Continue to save
- ❏ Continue to pay down debts

About a Year Before You Enter the Fulfilling Stage . . .

- ❏ Choose your expected start date
- ❏ Set up your budget based on estimated expenses and income replacement ratio
- ❏ Consider consolidating some of your retirement accounts
- ❏ Determine if you'd like to work (e.g., new career, part-time, consulting, etc.)
- ❏ Set your Fulfillment Stage goals (and discuss them with your spouse or partner)

A Few Months Before You Enter the Fulfilling Stage . . .

- ❏ Inform your employer you intend to cease work and fill out the necessary paperwork
- ❏ Talk with human resources about your retirement plan options and/or stock options
- ❏ Ask for an income estimate from your pension company (if applicable)
- ❏ Create a withdrawal strategy that helps ensure your income will last all the years you live in retirement
- ❏ Apply for Medicare if it is three months before your 65th birthday

❑   Set an age to begin taking Social Security
❑   Consider meeting with a tax adviser and/or attorney to map out your tax strategy and/or estate plan

Enter the Fulfillment Stage!

❑   Congratulations! Pat yourself on the back!
❑   Have a party!

After You Entered the Fulfillment Stage . . .

❑   Continue to follow your income strategy
❑   Reevaluate your goals and income strategy as your circumstances change
❑   Routinely review your beneficiaries to ensure they are correct and up to date
❑   Work with your tax professional to take care of your tax obligations and watch for IRS forms/reporting issues

After completing the worksheet and checklists, how prepared do you feel? What things can you do now to live comfortably in the Fulfillment Stage later? What questions do you have?

_____

_____

_____

_____

_____

_____

_____

_____

Whether you are years, months, or days away from entering the Fulfillment Stage, a financial professional can help answer many of your questions and offer useful tips.

Please note that a financial professional with an insurance license only may not do financial planning. Please ask your financial professional about whether he/she has the licensing to help with financial planning.

This informational publication is designed to provide general information on the subjects covered. Pursuant to IRS Circular 230, it is not, however, intended to provide specific legal or tax advice and cannot be used to avoid tax penalties or to promote, market, or recommend any tax plan or arrangement. Please note that *The FinancialVerse*, its affiliated companies, and their representatives and employees do not give legal or tax advice. You are encouraged to consult your tax adviser or attorney.

Any transaction that involves a recommendation to liquidate a securities product, including those within an IRA, 401(k), or other retirement plan, for the purchase of an annuity or for other similar purposes, can be conducted only by individuals currently affiliated with a properly registered broker/dealer or registered investment adviser. If your financial professional does not hold the appropriate registration, please consult with your own broker/dealer representative or registered investment adviser for guidance on your securities holdings.

Annuities are designed to meet long-term needs for retirement income. They provide guarantees against the loss of principal and credited interest, and the reassurance of a death benefit for beneficiaries.

Not affiliated with the US government or a governmental agency.

This informational publication is not approved, endorsed, or authorized by the Social Security Administration.